The Instructional Leader's Guide to **Implementing K-8 Science Practices**

The Instructional Leader's Guide to **Implementing K-8 Science Practices**

Rebecca **Lowenhaupt**
Katherine L. **McNeill**
Rebecca **Katsh-Singer**
Benjamin R. **Lowell**
Kevin **Cherbow**

ascd

Alexandria, Virginia USA

1703 N. Beauregard St. • Alexandria, VA 22311-1714 USA
Phone: 800-933-2723 or 703-578-9600 • Fax: 703-575-5400
Website: www.ascd.org • Email: member@ascd.org
Author guidelines: www.ascd.org/write

Ranjit Sidhu, *CEO & Executive Director;* Penny Reinart, *Chief Impact Officer;* Genny Ostertag, *Senior Director, Acquisitions and Editing;* Susan Hills, *Senior Acquisitions Editor;* Julie Houtz, *Director, Book Editing;* Jamie Greene, *Editor;* Thomas Lytle, *Creative Director;* Donald Ely, *Art Director;* José Coll, *Graphic Designer;* Kelly Marshall, *Production Manager;* Valerie Younkin, *Senior Production Designer;* Shajuan Martin, *E-Publishing Specialist*

All web links in this book are correct as of the publication date below but may have become inactive or otherwise modified since that time. If you notice a deactivated or changed link, please email books@ascd.org with the words "Link Update" in the subject line. In your message, please specify the web link, the book title, and the page number on which the link appears.

PAPERBACK ISBN: 978-1-4166-3054-8   ASCD product #122008   n10/21
PDF E-BOOK ISBN: 978-1-4166-3055-5; see Books in Print for other formats.

Quantity discounts are available: email programteam@ascd.org or call 800-933-2723, ext. 5773, or 703-575-5773. For desk copies, go to www.ascd.org/deskcopy.

Library of Congress Cataloging-in-Publication Data
Names: Lowenhaupt, Rebecca, author. | McNeill, Katherine L., author. | Katsh-Singer, Rebecca, author. | Lowell, Ben, author. | Cherbow, Kevin, author.
Title: The instructional leader's guide to implementing K-8 science practices / Rebecca Lowenhaupt, Katherine L. McNeill, Rebecca Katsh-Singer, Ben Lowell, Kevin Cherbow.
Description: Alexandria, VA : ASCD, [2022] | Includes bibliographical references and index.
Identifiers: LCCN 2021025317 (print) | LCCN 2021025318 (ebook) | ISBN 9781416630548 (paperback) | ISBN 9781416630555 (pdf)
Subjects: LCSH: Science—Study and teaching (Elementary) | Science—Study and teaching (Middle school) | Science—Study and teaching—Supervision. | Science teachers—In-service training.
Classification: LCC LB1585 .L65 2022 (print) | LCC LB1585 (ebook) | DDC 372.35/044—dc23
LC record available at https://lccn.loc.gov/2021025317
LC ebook record available at https://lccn.loc.gov/2021025318

30 29 28 27 26 25 24 23 22   1 2 3 4 5 6 7 8 9 10 11 12

The Instructional Leader's Guide to Implementing K–8 Science Practices

Acknowledgments......................................vii

Introduction 1

1: The Science Practices: A Primer.........................9

2: A Framework for Supervision: The Continuum................27

3: The Supervision Cycle 43

4: Observation.......................................58

5: Feedback 75

6: Professional Development.............................92

7: Taking the First Steps 108

Appendix A..115

Appendix B..123

Appendix C..125

References...134

Index...137

About the Authors...................................141

Acknowledgments

This material is based on work supported by the National Science Foundation under grant DRL-1415541. This four-year project consisted of the research and development of resources to support instructional leaders with the science practices in the Next Generation Science Standards (NGSS). Any opinions, findings, conclusions, or recommendations expressed in this material are those of the authors and do not necessarily reflect the views of the National Science Foundation.

Our team did not do this alone. We want to thank Kyle Fagan and Megan McKinley-Hicks for their contributions to the study at the outset, as well as the advisors and mentors who helped us design the project. Throughout, we have all relied on the support of our partners, children, and families as we engaged in this project. We want to share our love and gratitude with them.

Finally, we want to acknowledge the many contributions to the project made by our partners in the field, especially the principals and instructional leaders who helped us develop and refine the materials we share in this book. Without their dedication and commitment to improving their own practice, we would not have been able to co-create the tools to help others take up this important and challenging work.

Introduction

Unlike other professions, teachers in recent years have been continuously asked to change their daily routines and practices—often abruptly and with little training. Imagine a baker who has been at it for decades, rising early, gathering and mixing ingredients, and methodically kneading and baking bread. The baker eventually becomes an expert after years of practice. Over time, the recipe has been tweaked and the timing has been adjusted, but the basic steps and rhythms remain the same. How often do we ask an expert baker to abruptly switch gears, drop the old routine, and pivot to making soup or ice cream or something completely different?

Through an onslaught of instructional policies, public school teachers have been asked to remake their daily classroom routines multiple times in response to various standards-based reforms, curriculum changes, and technologies that have upended classroom life. These demands often come with little support, training, or time for preparation. At the same time, teachers have been criticized for digging in their heels and refusing to change.

Don't get us wrong—many of these policies push for necessary improvements to classrooms, which have stubbornly maintained the same structure and routines over time, despite substantial changes in our society. We just feel it is important to acknowledge that what is being asked of teachers and those who support them is no small task. Teachers are being asked to fundamentally change their ways of doing things—so they need guidance, patience, and time to do so. Several scholars have highlighted the many ways reform can go awry if those tasked with implementing it do not fully understand it or have opportunities to reflect on how the new approach fits with their current understanding and practice (Coburn, 2006; Cohen, 1990; Spillane, 2009). At the same time, we know that with support, teachers can and do learn new ways of doing things. Just look at the varied and innovative responses to school closure and remote learning during the COVID-19 pandemic for powerful examples of teachers enacting meaningful change.

Instructional leaders can be the source of this support, but they often lack the knowledge, time, and strategy to help teachers navigate the many changing demands of the classroom. As they support professional learning, evaluate teachers, help them set goals, and adopt new curricula, instructional leaders may not fully understand the reforms they aim to help teachers implement. They, too, need to learn new strategies for their work as they take on ambitious reform that seeks to transform traditional workings in the classroom.

One such reform involves a reconceptualized approach to K–8 science instruction in the form of the Next Generation Science Standards (NGSS). Currently underway in various forms across the country, implementation of the NGSS requires an overhaul of science instruction that not only takes on new content but also introduces the Science and Engineering Practices (SEP), a set of key skills that span the grades and provide students with the experience of doing science in much the same way as scientists do. These eight practices—including Planning and Carrying Out Investigations, Analyzing and Interpreting Data, and Engaging in Argument from Evidence—shift the learning of science away from the study of known facts to participating in the process of science. Especially at the K–8 level, this requires a substantial change to classrooms and the role of the teacher, who no longer delivers scientific knowledge but rather scaffolds exploration as students construct their own knowledge by engaging in the practices.

As a lower-stakes subject (compared to mathematics and literacy), science has long been overlooked as a focus for instructional leadership. Indeed, the narrowing of the curriculum to focus primarily on tested subjects has left many K–8 schools with less time in the schedule for science and even less support for improving science instruction (Lowenhaupt & McNeill, 2019). This marginalization of science in K–8 schools has often been explained by the misperception that students need to first develop their mathematics and literacy skills before they can engage in science learning.

In this context, many leaders have focused their efforts instead on supporting teacher learning in the fields of mathematics and literacy and left teachers on their own to determine how best to enhance and deliver science instruction. As districts and schools adopt the NGSS, they are finding that there is not the same depth and sophistication in the available resources and tools than what has been developed for instructional leadership in other subjects. Even as more robust supervision systems have been created to ensure greater support and accountability in teacher evaluation, these systems have tended to approach teacher evaluation from a content-neutral perspective rather than providing instructional leaders with subject-specific tools to use as they observe, provide feedback, and develop professional learning opportunities for teachers.

The ILSP Project and Who We Are

In this book, we share the tools and insights from the Instructional Leadership for Science Practices (ILSP) project. Our work started with a conversation between two of this book's coauthors in a coffee shop. Katherine McNeill and Rebecca Lowenhaupt identified a need at the intersection of instructional leadership and science reform. In her class on instructional leadership, Rebecca had struggled to find resources that were subject-specific as she compiled observation protocols for students. Katherine spoke with enthusiasm about her work on the SEP and efforts to train teachers in the NGSS, but she worried about the implementation process. She knew many school principals did not understand the purpose of or meaning behind the reform.

In working with K–8 principals, Rebecca and Katherine have found that many do not feel confident about their own understanding of science instruction. Most find supervising mathematics or literacy to be much more in their wheelhouse and speak about themselves as former science students who never really "got science." We recognize that without experience or confidence in science, these leaders are unlikely to tackle the implementation of the NGSS with the commitment it would require to support teachers. Nevertheless, we also know that with the right support, resources, and tools, many principals would be able to develop their instructional leadership for science. After all, principals don't need to be experts in science instruction; they just need to provide the focus, scaffolding, and opportunity for teachers to learn a new approach to their classroom.

Responding to this need, we created the Instructional Leadership for Science Practices study. With funding from the National Science Foundation and in collaboration with K–8 principals in the Boston area, we developed a set of tools and resources primarily targeting elementary and K–8 principals who have little subject expertise in science. Even those with a background in science are often unfamiliar with the approach outlined in the NGSS, but we were particularly committed to identifying key components of the science classroom that instructional leaders needed to attend to during their supervision process.

Our work centers on the science practices, the backbone of that reform. For each of the practices, we developed a continuum, instructional strategies, and essential insights to help leaders understand what they looked like in the classroom. Through workshops with principals, we created usable rubrics, observation forms, and feedback protocols to support the supervision process. We also designed professional development materials for principals to use as they worked alongside teachers to deepen their own understanding of the science practices.

The authors of this book have all been deeply engaged in the project, most of us since its inception in 2015. Rebecca and Katherine serve as the lead researchers and developers on the project with the help of several science specialists who are (or were) doctoral students in science education. A former science teacher, Katherine has made important contributions to the field as a professor of science education, but until this project, she had little experience with leadership. By contrast, Rebecca, an associate professor of educational leadership, brings her knowledge of instructional leadership and the supervision cycle to the study. A former English teacher, she has no direct expertise in science or science education, but she provides important perspectives as a non-science leadership person. Rebecca Katsh-Singer has continued to engage with the project in her role as the science curriculum coordinator for the Westborough School District in Westborough, Massachusetts. A former science teacher and coach, she has served as an instructional leader and engaged directly in K–8 science supervision, implementing the SEPs. Both Kevin Cherbow and Ben Lowell are former science teachers who currently work with Katherine on a science curriculum known as the OpenSciEd project (www.openscied.org). As a team, we bring together our various experiences working with teachers, principals, coaches, and other instructional leaders as well as our commitment to continue learning from and with those in the field.

Throughout the study, we collaborated closely with current K–8 school principals in urban, suburban, and rural school districts around Massachusetts. These principals, working in K–5, middle, and K–8 schools of different sizes, helped us understand the practical realities and challenges they face in their roles. These principals wear many hats and juggle a never-ending set of responsibilities, yet they share a commitment to improve science instruction in their schools—even though many lacked science expertise when we began our project. With their help, we were able to create a set of resources that address their unique needs, align with the existing tools they use, and provide support for them in their work with teachers.

As one principal who participated in our workshop put it, "As a vice principal (with a special education background) in a K–8 school, my level of expertise in the science curriculum is limited to what I taught in 2nd grade and what I observed while supporting students in other grades. This project gave me tremendous insight and understanding of science practices that I can apply to every grade level. It provided me with models of interacting with teachers during post observations and better formats for writing evaluations." Another principal explained, "The tools, videos, and transcripts from actual lessons grounded our learning in real-life examples, which enabled us to understand and picture the scientific practices much more effectively than just reading, listening, and discussing definitions."

We hope that you, the readers of this book, will find the same benefits as you adapt these resources for your own use in your unique school contexts.

A Central Assertion: Subject–Specific Supervision

At the heart of our work is a commitment to deepen our understanding of the content-specific features of science that warrant particular attention in the supervision process. Supervision at the K–8 level typically covers all subject areas, with teacher evaluation systems focused on general educators who teach across multiple subjects. Often, this leads to a content-neutral approach to supervision that emphasizes general pedagogical features such as student engagement, cognitive load, or classroom management.

Although these are certainly important aspects of instruction to address, we argue that for substantive reform within content areas to take place, both instructional leaders and teachers need to focus on the particular features of that subject. This requires attending to what Shulman (1986) referred to as "pedagogical content knowledge," the knowledge of how to teach a given subject, anticipate common misconceptions, and select the most meaningful methods and examples for teaching the content specific to the subject. Even more specifically, Stein and Nelson (2003) posited that instructional leaders need to leverage the insights of leadership content knowledge (LCK), which is knowledge specific to the subject and how it is both taught and learned. They point out that most instructional leaders may already have deep LCK in one subject, yet they can also develop sufficient working knowledge in other subjects to support their supervision within those subjects. Our project set out to make explicit the LCK necessary for instructional leadership of the science practices and scaffold leaders' learning of that LCK through science-specific tools and resources for supervision.

It is important to note that some administrators may argue with this approach, referring to the old adage that "Good teaching is good teaching, and I know it when I see it!" Though this may be true, we would amend that adage to point out that good teaching is not necessarily good science teaching, especially as we try to implement new approaches to science via the science practices. Content-neutral approaches to supervision run the risk of focusing on general pedagogies that may be strong but may not address the specific subject being taught.

To highlight this, we share a story from early in the project. During a school visit, Rebecca shadowed the principal for an observation of a 3rd grade classroom during a science lesson on astronomy. Students eagerly sat cross-legged on a rug with their science notebooks as the teacher read a book about an astronaut in space. As she read, she asked her students to share their thoughts, connect the astronaut's experiences to their own, and predict what might happen next. She explained how to write notes by providing a structure for their notes, sentence starters, and key vocabulary on the board.

About 15 minutes into the half-hour lesson, Rebecca realized this was a very impressive literacy lesson, but it was not a science lesson at all! In the post-observation debrief, the principal mentioned that the teacher had employed the literacy strategies they had recently learned in a professional development session. She spoke of the dilemma she faced in providing feedback—on one hand, she wanted to congratulate the teacher for integrating the new strategies, but on the other hand, she needed to address the fact that this lesson was not an effective science lesson and did not teach the science content or practices she had hoped to see.

If the principal had taken a content-neutral approach to the observation, she would certainly have emphasized the strong organization, classroom management, and scaffolding of the instruction. However, because of her focus on the specific subject of science, she was able to use the observation as an opportunity to reflect on the science practices. With a good relationship with the teacher, she was able to share both her praise of the strong literacy lesson she observed and her critique about the need to design lessons that integrate the science practices.

Even though we agree that it is important to pay attention to content-neutral aspects of instruction, it cannot end there. Therefore, the ILSP study provides tools to help instructional leaders focus on the science practices throughout the supervision cycle—thus helping support implementation of science reform in their schools.

An Overview of This Book

In this book, we share the approach we took in the ILSP project and explain how to use the tools and resources we've developed. In Chapter 1, we begin with a detailed explanation of the science practices, which can serve as a primer for those new to this approach. We share some common challenges with them and discuss some useful groupings. We then turn, in Chapter 2, to a description of the Science Practices Continuum, which is an anchor resource for our work and serves as a rubric for guiding implementation and supervision.

In Chapter 3, we introduce our approach to supervision and the components of the supervision cycle, which we discuss in greater detail in the next three chapters: observation (Chapter 4), feedback (Chapter 5), and professional development (Chapter 6). In each chapter, we incorporate specific examples, practical tips, and questions for reflection. Finally, we end with general insights and conclusions in Chapter 7.

Throughout the book, we have embedded tools and resources to support instructional leaders' supervision of the science practices, and we refer to the partner website for additional resources (www.scienceprac ticesleadership.com). We hope these resources are valuable to you as you support your district, school, and/or teachers in this important effort to provide all students with rich science experiences in which they work together to make sense of the world around them.

1

The Science Practices: A Primer

Ms. Chavez is a principal in an urban elementary school. Currently, her school is focused on disciplinary literacy, and she told her teachers she was interested in observing lessons in content areas such as science. Ms. Chavez observes a kindergarten classroom where the teacher, Ms. Brown, is introducing a new science unit. Ms. Brown says to her class, "We are starting a new unit on forces and motion. A force is a push or a pull. When you use a larger force, like a larger push, an object will go farther." She writes the definition of the word *force* on a piece of chart paper. Then she adds—and explains—two drawings to the paper: one with a person giving a big push to a ball rolling a far distance and a second with a person giving a small push to a ball rolling a short distance.

Ms. Brown then tells her students, "We are all going to do an experiment to see how this works—how larger forces make things, like a ball, move farther." She passes out a straw and ping-pong ball to each student and then holds up her same supplies. She puts the ping-pong ball on the floor and says she will blow as hard as she can in the straw to make the ball move. She explains she is using a large force and then counts the number of floor tiles the ball moved: five tiles. She then has all students try the experiment independently. After students complete the trial, she has them raise their hands according to how many tiles the ball moved. For example, she asks, "How many of you moved the ball five tiles? Raise your hand." She records on a second piece of chart paper that 11 students' balls moved five tiles. She continues recording responses for all students, gathering data from the entire class.

Then she repeats the demonstration by blowing through the straw softly. This time, her ball moves only one tile. After students complete the same experiment, she again asks them to raise their hands to show how many tiles the ball moved. At the end of the class, she returns to her original chart paper and reads the definition again: "A force is a push or a pull. When you use a larger force, like a larger push, an object will go farther." Finally, she asks one student to share how the experiment was similar to the two pictures posted of a person pushing a ball.

After the classroom observation, Ms. Chavez reflects on the science lesson. She is excited to see science in a kindergarten classroom because she knows it is important to engage kids with science at a really young age. She is also pleased that the lesson was hands-on and that Ms. Brown used both text and images to illustrate the science ideas in multiple modalities. However, Ms. Chavez feels like there was something missing from the lesson. She knows the new science standards in her state include a focus on the science practices, so she wonders if they were represented in Ms. Brown's lesson. And if so, which ones? During her observation, she also noticed that some students were quiet and did not appear interested in the experimental procedure. She wonders if there might be a different way to engage these students in group discussions and in "doing" the science.

In this chapter, we introduce the science practices. We begin by discussing recent shifts in science standards and describing the science practices. Next, we describe how grouping the science practices can serve as a tool to analyze curriculum and classroom instruction. We use concrete examples from K–8 science classrooms to illustrate these groups of science practices. At the end of the chapter, we offer practical tips and return to Ms. Chavez's concerns to discuss how to shift classroom instruction to align with the science practices.

Theorizing the Science Practices: Figuring Out the Natural World

What Are the Science Practices?

The science practices are the language, tools, ways of knowing, and social interactions that scientists (and students) use as they construct, evaluate, and communicate science ideas. This view of science as practice originally stemmed from the variety of activities in which scientists engage, including specialized ways of reasoning, talking, and making sense of the world around them (Lehrer & Schauble, 2006). Focusing on the science practices offers a different vision of classroom instruction—a vision that moves beyond "learning about" science (i.e., memorizing facts) to "figuring out" the natural world using these different ways of reasoning and communicating (Schwarz, Passmore, & Reiser, 2017).

Specifically, A Framework for K–12 Science Education (the Framework; National Research Council, 2012) and the Next Generation Science Standards (NGSS; NGSS Lead States, 2013) include eight science practices (see Figure 1.1). Later in this chapter and throughout this book, we will include examples of each of these science practices to illustrate what they look like in classrooms. As a set, though, you can see that each practice includes actions or activities students should engage in as they build and use science ideas. This is a more student-directed and collaborative vision of science than some previous traditional approaches.

Each science standard in the NGSS includes both a science practice and a disciplinary core idea (i.e., science idea) because the two work together synergistically as students make sense of the world around them. Science instruction should not focus on only one science idea (e.g., understanding that a force is a push or a pull or describing the characteristics of a scientific model); rather, it should include the science practice and science idea working together. For example, one of the 4th grade NGSS standards states, "Develop a model to describe that light reflecting from objects and entering the eye allows objects to be seen" (4-PS4-2). The science practice in this standard is the second one listed in Figure 1.1: Developing and Using Models. The disciplinary core idea—or science idea—focuses on light reflecting off a surface and entering an eye to see an object. A science classroom targeting this standard should have students develop their own models about how they see objects as they build stronger understandings of light reflecting and eyesight.

FIGURE 1.1 : Eight Science Practices

1. Asking Questions
2. Developing and Using Models
3. Planning and Carrying Out Investigations
4. Analyzing and Interpreting Data
5. Using Mathematics and Computational Thinking
6. Constructing Explanations
7. Engaging in Argument from Evidence
8. Obtaining, Evaluating, and Communicating Information

Figure 1.2 includes specific definitions for each of the eight science practices. It is important to note that a number of these practices align with the disciplinary practices in English Language Arts and Mathematics contained in the Common Core State Standards (Cheuk, 2013). For example, Engaging in Argument from Evidence is a practice that is found across the disciplines. Connecting and building on these commonalities in other disciplines can help teachers and students in this important work. However, it is also important to keep in mind differences across the disciplines. For example, what counts as evidence in a science argument (e.g., data from observations and measurements) is different from evidence in English language arts (e.g., a quote from a text). Another example is that Developing and Using Models in science focuses on a representation that predicts or explains the natural world, which is different from other disciplines where the word *model* can be used to refer to an exemplar or demonstration.

FIGURE 1.2 : Definitions of the Eight Science Practices

Science Practice	Definition
Asking Questions	Scientific questions lead to explanations of how the natural world works and can be empirically tested using evidence.
Developing and Using Models	A *model* is an abstract representation of a phenomenon that is a tool used to predict or explain the natural world. Models can be represented as diagrams, 3D objects, mathematical representations, analogies, or computer simulations.
Planning and Carrying Out Investigations	An *investigation* is a systematic way to gather data (e.g., observations or measurements) about the natural world, either in the field or in a laboratory setting.
Analyzing and Interpreting Data	Analyzing and Interpreting Data includes making sense of the data produced during investigations. Because patterns are not always obvious, this includes using a range of tools such as tables, graphs, and other visualization techniques.
Using Mathematics and Computational Thinking	Mathematical and computational thinking involves using tools and mathematical concepts to address a scientific question.
Constructing Explanations	A *scientific explanation* is an explanatory account that articulates how or why a natural phenomenon occurs and how it is supported by evidence and scientific ideas.
Engaging in Argument from Evidence	*Scientific argumentation* is a process that occurs when there are multiple ideas or claims (e.g., explanations, models) to discuss and reconcile. An argument includes constructing a claim supported by evidence and reasoning as well as evaluating and critiquing competing claims.
Obtaining, Evaluating, and Communicating Information	Obtaining, evaluating, and communicating information occur through reading and writing texts as well as communicating orally. Scientific information needs to be critically evaluated and persuasively communicated as it supports engagement in the other science practices.

Two of the science practices include distinct language in relation to engineering, which we did not include in our definitions in Figure 1.2. Practice 1 includes "defining problems," and Practice 6 includes "designing solutions." These practices ask students to learn about not only the natural world but also the humanmade or engineered world around them. These engineering practices highlight the type of work that engineers do as they try to solve problems (Cunningham, 2017).

These engineering practices are related to the science practices, but they also include some distinct features and are not the focus of this book. If you're interested, there are other curricula (Engineering Is Elementary, 2011) and resources (Cunningham, 2017) focused on the distinct aspects of engineering and the designed world.

Science Practices and Equity

Including the science practices in classroom instruction can support an equity vision of science instruction in which each student is known, heard, and supported with access and opportunities for learning. Realizing the potential of the emphasis on science practices in recent standards "is particularly important in relation to students of color, students who speak first languages other than English, and students from low-income communities who, despite numerous waves of reform, have had limited access to high-quality, meaningful opportunities to learn in science" (Bang, Brown, Calabrese Barton, Rosebery, & Warren, 2017, p. 33). To support all students in science, we need to move away from traditional science instruction, which does not adequately address equity issues.

An emphasis on science practices can expand the sensemaking practices typically valued in classrooms as well as leverage the resources and interests students bring to their science classrooms. Research has shown that students from historically underserved communities can experience science class as disconnected from their lives and experiences (Bang et al., 2017). In a classroom focused on the science practices, instruction begins with students asking questions and investigating phenomena; it does not start with preteaching vocabulary or following prescribed steps in a science procedure. Furthermore, it engages students in a rich repertoire of practices such as arguing from evidence, constructing models, and communicating ideas. This opens more opportunities for students. As the Framework argues, "The actual doing of science or engineering can also pique students' curiosity, capture their interest, and motivate their continued study" (National Research Council, 2012, p. 42). Students can see science as a practice in which they have an opportunity to engage rather than as a set of predetermined facts or procedures they have to follow.

This work can start with students' direct experiences and empower them to use their own language and voice as they make sense of the world around them (Brown, 2019). As we discuss throughout this book, science begins with students asking questions about the natural world and the phenomena they experience in their science classrooms. By starting with this shared experience and with students' own questions, *all* students can feel more connected to and interested in science. In addition, when teachers attend to what students say and do in these spaces, they can build stronger relationships with their students (Bang et al., 2017). This focus on science practices can support the creation of more equitable and culturally responsive classroom environments in which more students see themselves as "science people" and build rich science ideas about the natural world. Consequently, a focus on the science practices supports more equitable classroom instruction.

Grouping the Science Practices into Investigating, Sensemaking, and Critiquing

At first, eight distinct practices can feel overwhelming, but they are not independent. Rather, they overlap and work together to support a new vision of science instruction in which students actively figure out the world around them (Bell, Bricker, Tzou, Lee, & Van Horne, 2012). To highlight this overlap and offer an entry point into the science practices, we cluster the practices into three groups. Figure 1.3 illustrates these groups of science practices and how they work together to support scientific sensemaking (McNeill, Katsh-Singer, & Pelletier, 2015).

In Figure 1.3, we see that the overarching goal of science is to make sense of the natural world. Scientists and students do this by engaging in investigating practices, which result in the collection of data (i.e., observations or measurements). After collecting the data, they then engage in sensemaking practices, which result in the development of explanations or models. Once they have initial explanations or models, they use critiquing practices to compare and evaluate competing explanations and models, which helps determine the strongest explanation or model and identify remaining gaps or questions that need further exploration.

FIGURE 1.3 : Three Groups of Science Practices:
Investigating, Sensemaking, and Critiquing

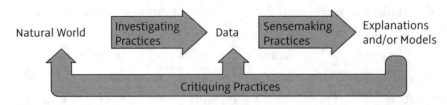

Source: A version of this figure appeared in "Assessing Science Practices: Moving Your Class Along a Continuum," by K. L. McNeill, R. Katsh-Singer, and P. Pelletier, 2015, *Science Scope, 39*(4), p. 22. Copyright 2015 by NSTA.

Figure 1.4 illustrates one way to organize the science practices according to these three groups: investigating, sensemaking, and critiquing. We acknowledge that there is no one right way to group the science practices. For example, a practice such as modeling could be placed in more than one group, depending on if the model is used to support students in asking questions or developing explanations of their data. However, these three groups can be productive conversation starters for initially exploring the science practices that are or are not occurring in K–8 science classrooms. Furthermore, they can be used to analyze curriculum or classroom instruction and help identify areas that need greater focus in a classroom, school, or district.

FIGURE 1.4 : Science Practices Organized into Three Groups

Investigating Practices	Sensemaking Practices	Critiquing Practices
1. Asking Questions 3. Planning and Carrying Out Investigations 5. Using Mathematics and Computational Thinking	2. Developing and Using Models 4. Analyzing and Interpreting Data 6. Constructing Explanations	7. Engaging in Argument from Evidence 8. Obtaining, Evaluating, and Communicating Information

Source: A version of this figure appeared in "Assessing Science Practices: Moving Your Class Along a Continuum," by K. L. McNeill, R. Katsh-Singer, and P. Pelletier, 2015, *Science Scope, 39*(4), p. 23. Copyright 2015 by NSTA.

The ILSP team used these three groups as part of a research study in which 26 K–8 principals were interviewed about the science instruction in their schools (McNeill, Lowenhaupt, & Katsh-Singer, 2018). As part of the interview, principals were asked to describe good science instruction they had observed in their schools, and the team coded their responses based on the three groups of science practices.

In the results, 77 percent of principals discussed investigating practices, 38 percent discussed sensemaking practices, and 12 percent discussed critiquing practices. The percentages add up to more than 100 percent because some principals' descriptions included more than one group and were coded for all the groups in their descriptions. In this example, we see less attention being paid to sensemaking and critiquing practices, which suggests that these areas might be important foci for future professional learning or curriculum selection for the K–8 schools included in this sample.

The following vignettes are taken from K–8 classrooms to illustrate the three different groups of science practices. We selected examples across different grades and science ideas to illustrate what a focus on science practices looks like in schools across time and science topics.

Investigating Practices, Grade 8: Asking Questions and Collecting Data About Why a Speaker Vibrates

The investigating practices focus on asking questions and investigating phenomena in the natural world. A phenomenon is an observable event that students can experience in some visual, auditory, or tactile way (Lowell & McNeill, 2019). It can include a firsthand experience, such as putting a bath bomb in water, or it can include a secondhand experience, such as watching a video of a volcanic eruption. Experiencing a phenomenon helps students engage in the three investigating practices (Asking Questions, Planning and Carrying Out Investigations, Using Mathematics and Computational Thinking), which in turn help students produce data they will continue to make sense of through the other science practices.

The following vignette is from Mr. Oliver's 8th grade class. Mr. Oliver is currently teaching a middle school science unit called "How can a magnet move another object without touching it?" (from www.openscied.org). This vignette illustrates his students' engagement in Asking Questions and Planning and Carrying Out Investigations as they build an understanding of magnetic forces and how they are affected by different factors, such as the type of material used for the magnet or the number of turns of wire in an electromagnet.

The unit begins with students observing a slow-motion video of a speaker as it plays music. Then students dissect speakers to explore their inner workings. Mr. Oliver uses these experiences to ask his students what questions they have—as well as what ideas they have to investigate those questions. First, he begins with questions. He asks each student to write down a couple questions they have on sticky notes about their observations. He then asks the class to share their questions out loud and adds them to a Driving Question Board (DQB) on a large piece of chart paper at the front of the room.

Mr. Oliver calls on one student, Landon, who reads his question: "Why is there a coil of wire in the speaker?" Tiffany says that she has a related question and shares, "Does it matter what type of metal the coil of wire is made of?" Mario adds that he also asked about the coil. He asks, "Does the number of coils matter in terms of how loud the speaker is?" Mr. Oliver comments that he loves these questions about the coil and it sounds like students want to investigate it as a class. Another student, Danika, agrees the coil is important, but she thinks it needs to be near the magnet to make the speaker work. Danika then reads her question: "Can the coil in the speaker make noise on its own or does it need a magnet?" The class continues sharing their questions and then works together to group them into different areas, such as investigating the coil and magnet.

The next day, Mr. Oliver gathers the students around the DQB, and they revisit their questions about the coil and magnet. He says that today he wants students to plan and carry out their own investigations in small groups to find out more about magnets and coils and how they interact with each other. He shows students a table that includes different materials they could use for their investigations (e.g., magnets, different types of wire, batteries, a compass). He then provides students with a graphic organizer to help them pick one question to investigate and think about what experimental variable they want to change, what they would control, and how they would measure the outcome. Each small group then gets to work selecting a question and planning their investigation.

In this vignette, we see Mr. Oliver provide students with experiences with a phenomenon (a speaker) to help them generate questions that can be answered through evidence. Furthermore, he uses different instructional strategies (revisiting the DQB, showing materials, having students work in groups, and providing a graphic organizer) to support students in designing an investigation that will provide data they can use to help explain how a speaker works.

Sensemaking Practices, Grade 5: Figuring Out Where Plants Get the Matter They Need to Grow

The sensemaking practices focus on making sense of data about phenomena by looking for patterns and relations to develop explanations and models. These practices encourage students to build and apply science ideas as they explain how and why phenomena occur. The sensemaking practices include three science practices: Developing and Using Models, Analyzing and Interpreting Data, and Constructing Explanations.

The following vignette highlights these practices. In this example, Ms. Butler is teaching a Next Generation Science Storyline curriculum titled "Why do dead things disappear over time?" (www.nextgen-storylines.org). This 5th grade unit begins with students watching a time-lapse video of a dead animal over time, which results in students generating many questions. Specifically, this vignette is from about halfway through a unit in which students are focused on plants and figuring out where plants get the matter they need to grow.

At the beginning of this science unit, Ms. Butler's 5th grade students had a variety of ideas about where plants get the matter they need to grow. They had previously learned in 2nd grade that matter comprises everything around them—it is anything that has mass and takes up space. But the students still have questions about whether some things are matter (Is light matter? Is air matter?), and they are unsure about what helps plants grow. The students' initial ideas about where plants might get the matter they need to grow include light, air, water, and soil. Ms. Butler uses students' questions to drive a series of investigations in which students collect data that demonstrate air and water are required for plant growth, whereas soil is not. They also collect data that show light is needed—but is not matter because light does not have mass. Finally, Ms. Butler wants to support her students in making sense of the data they collected and write a scientific explanation.

Ms. Butler shows her students two photos of an oak tree from in front of their school. One is from 20 years ago when the tree was small, and the other was taken the day before. She tells students she wants them to use the data they have been gathering in their science notebooks about where plants get matter they need to grow and write an explanation that addresses the following question: How has the oak tree in front of our school gotten so much larger over the last 20 years?

She then projects an explanation and explains that it is not very strong. It states, "The oak tree is a lot bigger because a lot of time has passed and the soil went into the tree and made it larger." She asks students to turn to a partner and critique this explanation. How could it be stronger? What should they include in their own explanations? After these partner discussions, Ms. Butler brings the class back together and asks students to share their ideas, which she records on a piece of chart paper. As a class, the students generate the following points:

1. Explain how the oak tree gets bigger.
2. Use evidence from our investigations.
3. Use science ideas we have learned about plants: Water and air are matter plants need to grow. Soil is not needed for growth. Light is not matter, but it is still necessary to grow.

After generating the list, Ms. Butler asks students to write their individual explanations.

In this vignette, we see Ms. Butler focus on one of the sensemaking practices—Constructing Explanations. She knows her students used investigating practices over the previous couple of weeks to collect a significant amount of data related to plant growth. Now she wants them to dig into and make sense of that information. She also wants to make sure her students connect the investigations they've done in class to plants outside the classroom. To support them in this work, she uses an example of a weak explanation and partner talk to help students think about what they learned and the goals for the science writing. She also uses a class-created list as a visual reminder for students to use as they construct and evaluate their own explanations.

Critiquing Practices, Grade 2: Arguing About Why the Shape of the Coast Has Changed

The critiquing practices emphasize that students need to compare, contrast, and evaluate competing explanations and models as they make sense of the world around them. Critique is a hallmark of scientific practice, but it has traditionally been absent from K–12 science instruction (Osborne, 2010). The critiquing practices include Engaging in Argument from Evidence and Obtaining, Evaluating, and Communicating Information.

Ms. Mitta's 2nd grade class is in the middle of a science unit focused on processes that shape Earth. She began the unit with videos and pictures of a locally relevant phenomenon for her students: images of coastal erosion showing land falling into the ocean. After her students generate a variety of questions, they collect data (e.g., using stream tables, using straws and sand, going on a field trip to observe the coast) and develop models to show how the coast is changing—and why. Her students draw their models in small groups during class. In reviewing the models, she realizes students have included different causes for the coastal change: water, wind, humans, or some combination thereof.

The next day, Ms. Mitta displays students' models at the front of the room. She explains that scientists often have multiple models, and they must consider the strengths and weaknesses of the models to then revise and strengthen them. She tells the class they are going to engage in argument using evidence to discuss the different models. She shows a poster with five sentence starters on it:

- My claim for what caused the change in the coast is…
- My evidence is…
- I think my evidence supports my claim because…
- I agree because…
- I disagree because…

She then has students sit in a circle so they are facing one another and starts the discussion. Ms. Mitta is impressed with her students' thoughtful ideas and how they use the models and evidence from their investigations to support their claims. By the end of the discussion, the class agrees that both water and wind cause erosion on the coast, and they use evidence from their stream table and straw investigations. Nevertheless, they have a lot of questions about the role and impact of humans in the process. Therefore, they decide they need to gather more evidence to decide whether humans should be in their model.

In this vignette, we see Ms. Mitta supporting her 2nd grade students in the critiquing practices. Specifically, she focuses on Engaging in Argument from Evidence and Communicating Information.

This vignette highlights that even early elementary students can engage in rich argumentation using evidence. Ms. Mitta included several instructional strategies to support her students in this work. For example, she organized the models so students could visually see there were differences across them in terms of the cause of the phenomenon. Then she provided students with sentence starters and purposefully arranged her classroom so students could see one another, the sentence starters, and the grouping of the models. Using different strategies can help create a classroom culture in which students can compare and critique different claims using evidence.

A Few Practical Tips

Familiarize Yourself with the Three Groups

In this chapter, we presented the recent shift in science education to focus on science practices, introduced the eight science practices, and provided three groups to reflect on those practices. We suggest using Figure 1.3 (p. 16) to think about the role of phenomena in the natural world, data, and explanations/models in relation to classroom science. The overarching goal of recent reform efforts is to shift K–12 science instruction from "learning about" science facts or terms to "figuring out" phenomena in the natural world. The science practices engage students in this critical work as students obtain data, construct explanations and models, and critique those explanations and models as they build and apply richer understandings of science ideas. We suggest familiarizing yourself with the three groups of science practices—investigating, sensemaking, and critiquing—as an entry point into this work. Initially, thinking about these three groups can be less overwhelming than considering all eight, and it can highlight the key goals across all science practices.

Use the Three Groups to Analyze Curriculum and Instruction

After familiarizing yourself with the three groups, you can then use the groups to critically look at the science instruction and curriculum in your school. Are there instructional activities or lessons focused on all three groups? Are some groups more prevalent than others across the curriculum or grade bands? For example, our research found that principals observed more instruction focused on the investigating practices than on the sensemaking or critiquing practices (McNeill et al., 2018). Discovering patterns such as this in your school's instruction or curriculum may suggest important areas of work for future professional learning opportunities.

Focus on One Group at a Time as Part of Professional Learning

Exploring all eight science practices at once in professional learning can be overwhelming for teachers. One strategy, after briefly introducing all eight science practices and the three groups, is to focus on one group at a time. Doing so can allow teachers to dig in and develop a richer understanding of each set of practices. Furthermore, it provides time for teachers to try out instructional strategies for each group and reflect with peers on the strengths and weaknesses of their approach and on what they are observing with their students. For example, a school could decide to focus on sensemaking practices because this is an area that has received little attention in the past and because some teachers found it was difficult for their students. This common focus can allow teachers to compare students' explanations and models across grades and discuss how different instructional strategies can be customized for the students in their school. (See Chapter 6 for more detailed recommendations about professional development.)

Returning to Ms. Chavez

After observing and reflecting on the kindergarten science lesson, Ms. Chavez decides to meet and talk with Ms. Brown. During their conversation, Ms. Chavez tells Ms. Brown she is excited to see science in her classroom and loves that she is engaging her students in this work. She then asks Ms. Brown what she feels the purpose or goal of the lesson was. Ms. Brown responds that it targets a science standard focused on planning and investigating to compare the effects of different strengths of pushes or pulls on the movement of an object (NGSS, K-PS2-1). She originally thought the lesson was aligned with that goal, but she indicates that she is also not completely satisfied with the science lesson. She feels her students can do more, and she is concerned that some of her students did not seem as engaged as she had hoped they would be.

Ms. Chavez shares Figure 1.4 (p. 16) with Ms. Brown, and the two discuss which of the three groups of science practices the lesson targeted. They both feel like it included a focus on the investigating practices but that the current design limited student choice and thinking. Ms. Brown suggests that next time she could use a short video of something the students were familiar with that included motion, such as part of a soccer game or kids playing on a playground. She could use that phenomenon to encourage students to generate their own questions and then have students work in groups to select a question to investigate. She could provide each group with a bag of materials (e.g., ping-pong ball, golf ball, rubber band, straw), which they could then use to design an investigation to explore the question.

Furthermore, instead of telling students at the start of the lesson that the larger the force or push, the farther an object would go, Ms. Brown could instead ask students to come to their own conclusions based on their data. She wants the lesson to be less about her giving the science ideas to her students and more about them actively figuring out those ideas together.

Discussion Questions

Reflection

1. How is the shift toward science practices similar to and different from previous reforms in science education?
2. How can shifting toward science practices support more equitable opportunities for all students in science?
3. Think about the vignettes used in this chapter. How were students engaged in the science practices? How does that compare to previous science instruction?

Application

1. How familiar are stakeholders in your school (teachers, parents) or district (administrators) with the recent shifts in science education toward science practices? What opportunities and challenges do you envision for supporting this shift?
2. How might you use the three groups of science practices in your school?

3. It can be overwhelming to focus on all eight science practices at once. If you were to select one group of science practices (investigating, sensemaking, or critiquing) to be the focus of professional development for your teachers, which would you select? Why?

2

A Framework for
Supervision: The Continuum

Principal Álvarez gets word over the summer that she will be leading a new science education reform effort in her K–8 school. Her district has recently adopted the Next Generation Science Standards, which were designed for students to engage in the science practices to figure out science ideas. She is now expected to provide instructional leadership to her science teachers as they enact these standards. To prepare for the beginning of the school year, Principal Álvarez reflects on how she has supervised different subjects in the past at her school. Supervising English language arts (ELA) always felt natural for her. She is a former ELA teacher and knows what good teaching looks like at each grade level. However, she has never taught science. Principal Álvarez is worried she cannot support her science teachers to teach these new standards effectively. She decides she needs more help to supervise her teachers in this new reform.

Looking for help, she first consults the observation protocols and supervision rubrics her district has given her. However, in reading them, she finds the tools are too general to help her supervise science instruction specifically. The protocols talk about things like student engagement but say little about science teaching and learning. Principal Álvarez continues her search until she comes across a supervision tool called the Science Practices Continuum. She sees that the continuum is designed specifically to supervise teachers in science practice–based instruction. She feels this tool could help her supervision, so she decides to dig more deeply into the continuum and consider how to use this tool in her instructional leadership.

In this chapter, we discuss the Science Practices Continuum and how it provides a framework for our vision of science instructional leadership. We introduce the continuum and explain how it was designed to support science supervision and instruction. We begin this chapter with a brief rationale for the role of the science practices and a science-specific evaluation framework for supervising science teaching.

Theorizing the Need for a Science–Specific Evaluation Framework

Recently, principals have been tapped to serve as instructional leaders for a variety of ambitious instructional reforms and accountability policies in their schools. As instructional leaders, principals typically conduct frequent formal and informal classroom visits to observe teaching and gather evidence and provide ongoing feedback to teachers to improve their instruction (Kraft & Gilmour, 2016; Marshall, 2013). Recent science reforms, such as the NGSS, necessitate that principals observe and provide science-specific feedback to teachers (Hill & Grossman, 2013). Therefore, principals' understanding of the subject they are supervising is integral to their efforts at subject-specific leadership (Nelson & Sassi, 2005; Spillane, 2005). However, principals rarely have a background or expertise in science (Halverson, Feinstein, & Meshoulam, 2011). As a result, it is unrealistic to expect that principals already possess the science content or leadership knowledge needed to effectively lead science reform in their schools (Lowenhaupt & McNeill, 2019).

Principals need to develop science-specific knowledge to support their instructional leadership of science. We have found that the NGSS science practices offer an important framework to support principals' understanding and supervision of science instruction in their schools (McNeill et al., 2018). The science practices offer a lens that principals can apply across grades, disciplines, and curriculum units because students engage in the practices across all these contexts. Therefore, the science practices are an accessible on-ramp for instructional leaders to deepen their understanding and capacity to supervise science instruction (McNeill et al., 2018).

In turn, the science practices are a powerful support in the design of science-specific supervision tools. Currently, there is a proliferation of resources to support instructional leaders' ongoing observation and feedback to their teachers (Bambrick-Santoyo, 2012). However, these resources, such as observation protocols (e.g., Danielson, 2007), largely focus on general pedagogical features such as student engagement (McNeill et al., 2018).

Therefore, we designed the Science Practices Continuum for principals to use in guiding and evaluating science practice–based instruction (McNeill et al., 2015). The continuum can be used by instructional leaders to assess student engagement in the science practices concerning these elements. Further, it provides leaders with science-specific language and an understanding of science instruction to use in their feedback to teachers to support their science teaching. As such, we believe the Science Practices Continuum is a valuable tool to support principals' leadership knowledge and practices for supervising science.

Understanding the Science Practices Continuum

We have created two versions of the continuum to help principals see and evaluate teachers' use of the science practices: one focused on supervision and the other focused on instruction. The supervision version of this tool centers on what teachers do to facilitate students' engagement in the science practices. The instruction version focuses on what students do themselves in their experience of the science practices.

Initially, we only created the supervision version of the continuum. We subsequently developed the instruction version based on feedback from the instructional leaders who initially used the supervision continuum. These leaders told us that they preferred to focus on student engagement rather than instruction during their supervision of science teaching. Consequently, we developed the instruction continuum to focus on students' engagement in the science practices. The two versions of the continuum are valuable for instructional leaders since they can train their eyes toward teachers or students, depending on their goals for supervising science.

In each version of the continuum, the practices are grouped into investigating, sensemaking, and critiquing practices (as discussed in Chapter 1). Each continuum illustrates four different levels of instruction or student engagement in each science practice (see Figure 2.1). The levels provide specific explanations of what the practices might look like at varying levels of proficiency. These levels are not grade-level specific, which provides flexibility for both teachers and instructional leaders. It gives teachers greater flexibility to teach in developmentally appropriate ways for any of the practices at any level. It also gives instructional leaders greater flexibility to use this tool in different science classrooms—the continuum can be readily applied across grade levels, science disciplines, and curricular units.

FIGURE 2.1 : A Continuum of Practices

	Level 1	Level 2	Level 3	Level 4
Investigating Practices				→
Sensemaking Practices				→
Critiquing Practices				→

The progression from Level 1 to Level 4 for each science practice is organized around several instructional elements. These instructional elements are embedded across each version of the continuum and constitute the key ideas or levers that distinguish the different levels for each science practice. A major goal in using the continuum is to highlight these key levers to supervise science instruction and help teachers move their teaching further along the continuum.

In this chapter, we highlight how the instructional elements and key levers are embedded in the supervision version of the continuum. We focus on the supervision continuum in this chapter but include both the supervision and instruction continuums in Appendix A. The instruction version of the continuum might be preferable or more useful for teachers, given its focus on students' engagement in the science practices.

Instructional Elements for the Science Practices

The Science Practices Continuum was designed around three core elements of instruction that support student engagement in science practices. Broadly, these elements are grounded in the recent reform shift in science education from students *learning about* science ideas to students engaging in science practices to *figure out* science ideas (Schwarz et al., 2017). We identified three instructional elements in the research literature that primarily constitute this shift in science education. Namely, it is (1) grounded in explaining natural phenomena, (2) focused on building and critiquing ideas using evidence, and (3) student-directed and collaborative. These three instructional elements are embedded across the science practices and levels and make up the key levers for each science practice row of the continuum.

The first element is *grounded in explaining natural phenomena*. Natural phenomena are observable events that occur in the universe (Lowell & McNeill, 2019). Grounding learning in natural phenomena allows students to engage in science practices to explain and predict those phenomena. Furthermore, grounding students' experiences in phenomena in the classroom can support more equitable science instruction as all students will have a common experience from which they can share their questions and ideas for investigation (Bang et al., 2017). From Level 1 to 4, we see a shift toward teachers facilitating students in the science practices to figure out natural phenomena.

The second element is *focused on building and critiquing ideas using evidence.* Scientific evidence includes data helpful in supporting a claim (used in an explanation or argument). When science teaching and learning are focused on building and critiquing ideas, students engage in science practices to seek, use, and evaluate evidence. From Level 1 to 4, we see a shift toward teachers facilitating and students engaging in the science practices to build, critique, and revise ideas based on scientific evidence (Osborne, 2010).

The third element is *student-directed and collaborative.* Student-directed science teaching and learning involve students engaged in science practices to make progress on their questions and ideas. Collaborative science teaching and learning involves students engaging in science practices together to make collective sense of ideas. This shift can also support more equitable science classrooms as it can increase engagement and empower students to have a voice in the direction of the science instruction. This can particularly support students who have not traditionally seen themselves as "science people" and help them see themselves as part of the classroom science community (Brown, 2019). From Level 1 to 4, we see a shift toward teachers facilitating students in the science practices in a manner that is directed by and equitable for all students.

Key Levers for the Science Practices

The instructional elements are reflected in the key levers for each science practice. These levers distinguish one level from another in each row and highlight a progression toward more complex engagement in the science practice. The key levers for each science practice represent the two or three elements that can be most challenging for teachers or students and are productive supports for shifting classroom culture toward prioritizing the science practices. These levers provide instructional leaders with valuable information to inform their supervision decisions and support teachers' facilitation of and students' engagement in greater proficiency of the focal practice. To highlight these key levers, we analyzed the levers for one science practice row from the continuum (see Figure 2.2).

At Level 1, teachers do not facilitate students in the science practice. At Level 2, teachers facilitate students in the science practice, but students' participation exhibits one or two of the common challenges identified in research literature. For example, in terms of asking questions, students ask both scientific and nonscientific questions. Scientific questions are distinct from other kinds of questions in that they can be answered through the gathering and interpretation of evidence about natural phenomena. Developing them is a common challenge for students. At Level 3, the teacher facilitates students effectively, but that facilitation is not primarily informed by critique. In other words, the teacher provides opportunities for students to ask scientific questions, but students are not given the opportunity to evaluate the merits and limitations of their questions. Finally, Level 4 describes teacher expertise in facilitating this science practice. The teacher facilitates opportunities for students to ask scientific questions about natural phenomena and to critique those questions.

FIGURE 2.2 : Continuum for Asking Questions

	Level 1	Level 2	Level 3	Level 4
Asking Questions	The teacher does not provide opportunities for students to ask questions.	The teacher provides opportunities for students to ask both scientific and nonscientific questions (i.e., not answerable through the gathering of evidence about natural phenomena).	The teacher provides opportunities for students to ask scientific questions (i.e., answerable through the gathering of evidence about natural phenomena). Students do not evaluate the merits and limitations of the questions.	The teacher provides opportunities for students to ask scientific questions. Students evaluate the merits and limitations of the questions.

Across the row, Asking Questions has two key levers. The first is whether the teacher provides opportunities for students to ask scientific questions, nonscientific questions, or no questions at all. This lever is constituted by the elements of natural phenomena and evidence, as these scientific questions are only answerable through the gathering of evidence about natural phenomena. The second lever is whether the teacher provides opportunities for students to evaluate one another's questions. This lever is grounded in evidence because at Level 4, teachers provide opportunities for students to build and critique their questions. Together, these levers provide instructional leaders and teachers with valuable information to support and inform instructional decisions that move students toward greater proficiency in Asking Questions.

Practice Interpreting the Continuum

Now that we have introduced and explained the components of the Science Practices Continuum, let's look at a few examples. In the following sections, we examine a science practice from each of the practice groupings introduced in Chapter 1: investigating, sensemaking, and critiquing. (See Appendix A for the supervision and instruction continuums.)

Part 1: Investigating Practice— Planning and Carrying Out Investigations

As you read through the continuum row shown in Figure 2.3, consider the following reflection questions:

- What are the key levers for this science practice? How do these levers progress across the continuum row?
- What instructional elements are included in this science practice? How are these elements present in the key levers you identified?

We found two key levers for the science practice of Planning and Carrying Out Investigations. The first involves how collaborative the investigation experience is for students. At Level 1, the teacher provides no opportunity for students to engage in investigations. At Level 2, this opportunity is teacher-directed, as the teacher plans and directs students in the investigation. At Level 3, students are given the opportunity to plan or conduct investigations, and at Level 4, students are given the opportunity to plan *and* conduct investigations about natural phenomena. The second lever involves whether students are given the opportunity to make decisions that are consequential to the planning and carrying out of the investigation. At Level 2, students make no decisions about investigation methods or variables. By contrast, at Levels 3 and 4, students are given the opportunity to make decisions in the planning and conducting of the investigation.

FIGURE 2.3 : Continuum for Planning and Carrying Out Investigations

	Level 1	Level 2	Level 3	Level 4
Planning and Carrying Out Investigations	The teacher does not provide opportunities for students to design or conduct investigations.	The teacher provides opportunities for students to conduct investigations to confirm ideas they have learned about, but these opportunities are typically teacher-driven. Students do not make decisions about experimental variables or investigational methods (e.g., number of trials).	The teacher provides opportunities for students to design **or** conduct investigations to gather data about how or why a natural phenomenon occurs. Students make decisions about experimental variables, controls, and investigational methods.	The teacher provides opportunities for students to design **and** conduct investigations to gather data about how or why a natural phenomenon occurs. Students make decisions about experimental variables, controls, and investigational methods.

Across the row, the teacher provides more opportunities for students to plan and carry out the investigations and figure out natural phenomena. At Level 2, students complete investigations and come to findings they have already learned about from their teacher. At Levels 3 and 4, the teacher provides opportunities for students to plan and conduct investigations to explain how or why a natural phenomenon occurs. In addition, the teacher provides more student-directed and collaborative opportunities for students to engage in the investigations as you move across the row. At Level 2, the teacher provides opportunities for students to conduct investigations, but they are teacher-directed. At Levels

3 and 4, these investigations become more student-directed and collaborative as students make decisions about experimental variables, controls, and investigational methods.

Part 2: Sensemaking Practice— Developing and Using Models

As you read through the continuum row shown in Figure 2.4, consider the following reflection questions:

- What are the key levers for this science practice? How do these levers progress across the continuum row?
- What instructional elements are included in this science practice? How are these elements present in the key levers you identified?

FIGURE 2.4 : Continuum for Developing and Using Models

	Level 1	Level 2	Level 3	Level 4
Developing and Using Models	The teacher does not provide opportunities for students to create or use models.	The teacher provides opportunities for students to create or use models. The models focus on describing science ideas or natural phenomena. Students do not evaluate the merits and limitations of the model.	The teacher provides opportunities for students to create or use models focused on predicting or explaining natural phenomena. Students do not evaluate the merits and limitations of the model.	The teacher provides opportunities for students to create or use models focused on predicting or explaining natural phenomena. Students evaluate the merits and limitations of the model.

We found two key levers for the science practice of Developing and Using Models. The first involves the nature of the models that are developed and/or used—are they descriptive or explanatory, or are they not models at all? At Level 1, the teacher provides no opportunity for students to engage in modeling. At Level 2, this opportunity is descriptive; students are given the opportunity to develop a model that describes a science idea or a natural phenomenon. At Levels 3 and 4, students predict and explain phenomena with their models. The second key lever involves the evaluation of the models. At Levels 1–3, teachers do not position students to evaluate the merits and limitations of one another's models. At Level 4, teachers give students the opportunity to critique one another's models.

Across the row, the teacher provides more opportunity for students to engage with models to figure out—rather than describe—natural phenomena. For example, at Level 2, teachers provide students with opportunities to develop or use models that describe science ideas or natural phenomena. At Levels 3 and 4, students develop and/or use models to predict or explain natural phenomena. In addition, the teacher provides more opportunities for students to critique the models they develop and use as you move across the row. At Levels 2 and 3, the teacher positions students to build and use models but not critique those models. At Level 4, teachers give students the opportunity to evaluate the merits and limitations of one another's models.

Part 3: Critiquing Practice— Engaging in Argument from Evidence

As you read through the continuum row shown in Figure 2.5, consider the following reflection questions:

- What are the key levers for this science practice? How do these levers progress across the continuum row?
- What instructional elements are included in this science practice? How are these elements present in the key levers you identified?

We identified two key levers for the science practice of Engaging in Argument from Evidence. The first involves how students' arguments are constructed. At Level 1, there is no opportunity for students to construct arguments. At Level 2, students construct arguments with evidence or reasoning. At Levels 3 and 4, students are afforded opportunities to construct arguments with evidence and reasoning. The second key lever involves how teachers facilitate discussion with students. At Level 2, we see students engaged in teacher-directed discussion. At Level 3, we see teachers positioning students to share their arguments and respond by agreeing or disagreeing with one another's claims. However, the teacher provides little opportunity to build or critique these ideas. At Level 4, we see student-driven discourse and critique of one another's ideas.

FIGURE 2.5 : Continuum for Engaging in Argument from Evidence

	Level 1	Level 2	Level 3	Level 4
Engaging in Argument from Evidence	The teacher does not provide opportunities for students to engage in argumentation.	The teacher provides opportunities for students to engage in argumentation where they support their claims with evidence or reasoning, but the discourse is primarily teacher-driven, or there are not competing arguments for students to make (i.e., there are not two or more potential claims for students to argue about).	The teacher provides opportunities for student-driven argumentation where students support their competing claims about natural phenomena with evidence and reasoning. Students agree and disagree, but they rarely engage in critique.	The teacher provides opportunities for student-driven argumentation where students support their competing claims about natural phenomena with evidence and reasoning. Students critique competing claims and build on and question one another's ideas.

Across the row, the teacher provides more opportunity for students to build and critique arguments using scientific evidence and reasoning. At Level 2, we see students given the opportunity to construct arguments using only evidence *or* reasoning. At Level 3, we see arguments with evidence and reasoning, but students rarely engage in critique. Finally, at Level 4, we see arguments with evidence and reasoning and students engaged in critique and construction of ideas. Second, students are given more opportunities to construct arguments about natural phenomena as you move across the row. At Levels 1 and 2, students are constructing arguments that are not grounded in figuring out a natural phenomenon. At Levels 3 and 4, teachers position students to make claims directly about how or why a natural phenomenon occurs. Finally, across the row, the teacher provides more opportunities for students to engage in student-driven and collaborative argumentation. At Level 2, argumentation discourse is primarily directed by the teacher. At Levels 3 and 4, this discourse becomes more student-driven. Further, at Level 4, students' engagement is fully collaborative as they direct their arguments to one another and critique and build on one another's claims.

A Few Practical Tips

Begin by Digging into the Continuum and Science Practices

The Science Practices Continuum and the NGSS science practices ground the use of our other supervision, instruction, and professional development tools. For example, our Observation Form (discussed in Chapter 4) and Post-Observation Conference Worksheet (discussed in Chapter 5) involve observing and providing feedback to teachers as they use the continuum tool. We think it is important that instructional leaders become well acquainted with the continuum and science practices before attempting to use any of the other tools.

We suggest that school leaders work through each continuum row describing the key levers and elements embedded in the row. In reviewing these rows, we also advise instructional leaders to consult Appendix C, which includes a set of instructional strategies associated with each of the science practices. This science practice–specific information can help leaders better understand the key levers or instructional elements in the context of a particular science practice. As a result, greater understanding of the key levers and elements supports more effective use of the continuum with our other tools and supports.

Reach a Consensus About the Continuum Version You Will Use

We developed the supervision and instruction versions of the continuum to give instructional leaders the flexibility to focus on teachers or students in supervising science at their schools. We have found that school leaders often gravitate toward one version or the other and rarely use both versions simultaneously. Further, we found that leaders empha-sized the decision of which continuum version to use with their science teachers. This decision is often based on how these leaders and their teachers typically frame instructional improvement at their schools (i.e., improving teaching or learning). As a result, we suggest that instruc-tional leaders come to a consensus with their science teachers about which continuum they will use. This consensus is important because it puts instructional leaders and science teachers on the same page with respect to observation and feedback.

Meet and Support Teachers Where They Are on the Continuum

It is important to consider how you will use the continuum to sup-port your teachers' instruction of science practices. We have found that it is not productive to frame instructional leadership around a desire to see teachers consistently achieve Level 4 ratings on the continuum. First, it's just a fact that not all science teaching will be at Level 4. This is nor-mal! It takes a lot of time and effort to build toward Level 4 engagement in any science practice.

Second, in many school contexts, it is unrealistic for teachers to initially achieve Level 4 for many science practices. Teachers may be unfamiliar with the practices themselves or may not currently have the resources (e.g., time, curriculum) to enact them effectively with their stu-dents. As a result, we find it much more productive to use the continuum to meet and support teachers where they are for a particular science practice. We suggest using the continuum to identify the teachers' cur-rent level for a practice and then provide feedback to help move their future instruction farther along the continuum from that point.

Returning to Principal Álvarez

After digging into the continuum, Principal Álvarez decides she wants to use it with her science teachers. Before the start of the year, she meets with them as a team to discuss the continuum. She highlights each version of the continuum, and they come to a consensus on using the instruction version. They then work together to identify the key levers and instructional elements for one science practice from each grouping in the continuum. During this work, Principal Álvarez has her teachers consult the science practice definitions for the rows they are analyzing. This supports the teachers' identification and description of the key levers and elements for these practices.

The meeting ends with Principal Álvarez giving her science teachers two homework assignments. First, they are to review the remaining continuum rows for the key levers and instructional elements. Second, they are to evaluate which science practices are currently present in their teaching—and at which level. Principal Álvarez plans to meet with each teacher in one-on-one settings to discuss this homework and to plan how to progress their instruction along the continuum during the coming school year. As a result of this preparation and planning, she starts the year more prepared to lead the science reform in her school.

Discussion Questions

Reflection

1. What are two take-aways for you from this chapter?
2. Think about the tools you currently use to supervise science teaching. Do they focus on science instruction specifically? How do these tools help and/or hinder your efforts to supervise science instruction at your school?
3. How might the Science Practices Continuum benefit your science-specific instructional leadership?
4. Think about the science teaching at your school. Which science practices do you think are most frequently taught in your school? At what level on the Science Practices Continuum are they typically taught? What science practices are not usually taught in your school? Why do you think that is?

Application

1. How do you plan to use the Science Practices Continuum to supervise science and improve science instruction at your school?
2. What will you do to help your teachers use the ideas and language of the continuum in their teaching and goal setting?
3. Which science practices will you focus on with your teachers? Why these practices? How will you help your teachers deeply understand these rows of the continuum?

3

The Supervision Cycle

At the start of the school year, Principal Thompson asks all the teachers to set up one-on-one meetings with her to discuss their goals for the year. Across Jackson Elementary, she hopes to help teachers integrate the science practices into their instruction as part of the district's push to implement the Next Generation Science Standards. Prior to the beginning of the school year, the teachers spent their professional development day learning about the standards and working in grade-level teams to plan science units.

In her meeting with Ms. Martinelli, a 2nd grade teacher, she learns that the teacher is unsure about how to integrate the science practices into her science teaching. Principal Thompson suggests she begin by focusing on the investigating practices, which include the practices of Asking Questions, Planning and Carrying Out Investigations, and Using Mathematical and Computational Thinking.

She says, "It looks like the district is offering a professional development session next week on planning investigations for the younger grades. Why don't you attend and see if you can bring back some ideas to your classroom?"

After she returns from the session, Ms. Martinelli stops by the principal's office to let her know that she plans to integrate an investigation into the unit on plants next week. Principal Thompson goes to observe that class and, during her 15-minute visit to the room, notices students working in small groups and preparing their materials according to procedures Ms. Martinelli has written on the board. She also observes Ms. Martinelli circulating around the room and helping students with the steps of the process, as necessary.

Theorizing the Supervision Cycle

This vignette illustrates how supervision can be enacted as an iterative cycle with observation, feedback, and ongoing professional learning. Even though Principal Thompson does not know all the answers about science instruction, she is able to facilitate the teacher's learning by providing some key insights based on her understanding of the Science Practices Continuum, engaging in reflective conversation, and ensuring the teacher has access to relevant support and resources. By approaching supervision as a learning opportunity, instructional leaders encourage teachers to work toward goals that align with schoolwide improvement efforts. Although supervision can be viewed primarily as a form of accountability, conceptualizing supervision as an ongoing learning cycle can foster development and growth among teachers, which can lead to instructional improvement (Sergiovanni, Starratt, & Cho, 2014). As illustrated in Figure 3.1, the cycle incorporates observation, feedback, and professional learning in a repeated, iterative process.

Historically, supervision has not always served this purpose. Traditional forms of supervision provided infrequent observations, which primarily served as basic benchmarks of teacher performance for accountability purposes (Marshall, 2013; Sergiovanni et al., 2014). Typically a series of checkmarks and lists that evaluators used only once every few years, these forms of supervision were often superficial gatekeepers that did not provide constructive feedback to teachers or meaningful levers for instructional reform. In recent years, the purpose of supervision has shifted to incorporate formative approaches to supporting teacher growth through more frequent observations, feedback, and professional learning opportunities (Lowenhaupt & McNeill, 2019; Sergiovanni et al., 2014). Although it continues to serve an important role in evaluation, many have viewed this cycle as a mechanism for implementing instructional policy and reform (Rigby et al., 2017).

FIGURE 3.1 : The Supervision Cycle

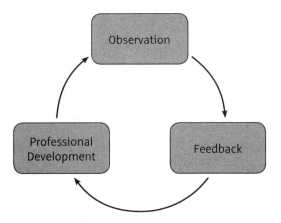

Coupling teacher evaluation and professional learning has helped promote instructional improvement and reform, but it can also lead to dilemmas about the need for accountability versus the goal of fostering growth and development. Encouraging teachers to try new things while they are evaluated on those new approaches can backfire if there are not strong relationships and supports in place. The supervision cycle ensures that teachers have access to training, opportunities to practice, and ongoing feedback over time. By building this continuous relationship, the weight of any one observation in the evaluation process is minimized. Ideally, educators should have a range of opportunities to show their expertise in some domains and growth in others.

As the purpose of supervision has evolved, the field has generated several approaches to observation and feedback that provide ongoing, specific, and actionable insights for teachers (e.g., Marshall, 2013). Several rubrics for supervision, such as the Danielson Framework (Danielson, 2007) or the Structured Immersion Observation Protocol (Echevarria, Vogt, & Short, 2016), have become essential tools for instructional leaders to use in their work with teachers. These rubrics are often formalized as part of the official evaluation process, providing frameworks for decisions about teacher contracts and assignments. At the same time, they offer important scaffolding for ongoing teacher development and help structure the supervision cycle.

These rubrics tend to provide content-neutral approaches to instructional improvement, emphasizing underpinning aspects of instruction that span the subject areas (Lowenhaupt & McNeill, 2019). Of course, as previously mentioned, there are always those who like to say, "Good teaching is good teaching, and I know it when I see it!" At some moments, this is certainly true. Although crucial for general evaluation processes and holistic teacher development, it is also important to provide teachers with content-specific frameworks that can focus instructional leaders and teachers on disciplinary particulars. Without these, it is difficult to help teachers develop a pedagogy for specific subjects and adopt new approaches within those subjects (such as implementing the science practices). Content-neutral supervision also runs the risk of leaving both supervisors and teachers with major gaps in their approach to specific subjects. Our work addresses these issues by providing science-specific tools for the supervision cycle. As leaders engage in science supervision specifically, they can use the Science Practices Continuum and other tools to support their focus on the science practices throughout the supervision cycle.

In an iterative cycle, it is important to consider where to begin the process. The answer to this question, like most in education, is "It depends!" For those just beginning to implement the science practices, we recommend introducing everyone to the practices and establishing a schoolwide commitment to focus on a few practices at a time (see Chapter 6 for our discussion of professional development). Utilizing the groupings laid out in Chapter 2, a good starting point may be the investigating practices, which likely align more closely than the other groupings to current practices.

As with all adult learning, the key is to build on existing knowledge and provide opportunities for teachers to consider how these "new" practices relate to and fit in with what they already know and do in their science instruction. Although for some, a schoolwide professional learning opportunity is a natural first step in the process, it may be important to begin with instructional leaders conducting classroom observations to identify the focus for professional learning. This also gathers information about current science instruction that will help identify the best entry point and plan a meaningful professional learning experience.

Implementing the supervision cycle requires leaders to approach the process with a growth mindset about both educators' and their own learning. Recognizing that teachers are learners allows leaders to think about supervision as an opportunity to foster teacher development— rather than as a purely evaluative process (Glickman, 2002). We also encourage instructional leaders to position themselves as learners. The science practices are new for most of us, and we need to continue developing our understanding of how they look in different classrooms, for different groups of students, and across grade levels.

As leaders prepare to engage in the supervision cycle, it's a good idea to reflect on the school's existing structures, schedule, and routines that can be leveraged in the service of learning to integrate the science practices. Districts often offer subject-specific expertise, such as a science director who might contribute to efforts to create meaningful and sustained teacher learning opportunities. For example, critical friends groups (Curry, 2008) and professional learning communities (DuFour & Eaker, 2009) may offer existing structures that instructional leaders can leverage for developing an understanding of the science practices.

We encourage leaders to take stock of the range of expertise, experiences, and motivations teachers bring to the science classroom. As Knight (2008), Jackson (2013), and others have highlighted, it is crucial to differentiate support for teachers, just as teachers do for their students. As we discuss further in this chapter, educators will land at different places on the "Will/Skill Continuum" (Jackson, 2013). Some will be eager to engage in professional learning, and others will be resistant. Some will have many strengths, and others with lower skill levels will need more support. By planning a schoolwide strategy, assessing the range of educators in the building (based on this continuum), and ensuring a focus on the science practices, leaders can make sure everyone benefits from engaging in the supervision cycle.

Three Stages of the Cycle

By actively engaging teachers in the supervision process, instructional leaders can build trust and strengthen relationships that will help facilitate ongoing learning. The three steps of the supervision cycle should inform one another and provide iterative and focused implementation of the science practices. Working with teachers both individually and collectively, instructional leaders can establish and work toward professional learning goals that align with each stage of the process. They should plan an approach to supervision that links each stage to the next and provides ongoing opportunities for learning that are aligned with observation and feedback. With each rotation through the supervision cycle, instructional leaders have an opportunity to improve instruction at each stage of the cycle.

Observation

Observations should be integrated into each supervision cycle so instructional leaders can see how teachers are taking up new instructional approaches they are learning. Leaders are most effective if they conduct frequent, targeted observations that hold a mirror up for teachers to see how they are doing and how they might continue to improve in specific and focused ways (Lowenhaupt & McNeill, 2019; Marshall, 2013). Implementing the science practices requires observations that focus on particular practices and content-specific features of instruction. In the best-case scenario, observers and teachers work together through the cycle to fully implement the science practices. Observation allows both supervisor and teacher to gather evidence of how it is going in the classroom and then use the feedback process to reflect on how things went and identify what might be improved. Chapter 4 lays out the approach we take to the observation stage of the cycle in more detail.

Feedback

Providing specific, actionable feedback that is focused on the target of observation serves as a crucial step in the supervision cycle (Bambrick-Santoyo, 2012). This allows an opportunity for reflection about the successes and challenges experienced during efforts to implement the science practices. Although feedback sessions can often seem one-directional as instructional leaders share their critiques and demands with teachers, we encourage using structured protocols that ensure two-way communication and provide an opportunity for authentic dialogue about the learning process.

This back-and-forth conversation can also help instructional leaders learn. Anchoring this conversation in the continuum can support collaborative conversation about how to implement the science practices most effectively, and it can depersonalize the feedback session by directing the conversation toward analysis in relation to a specific focus. In Chapter 5, we describe how we approach the feedback stage of the supervision cycle. This step of the cycle can help leaders plan for professional learning based on questions raised in the feedback session and determine the schedule and focus for the next classroom observation.

Professional Development

The professional learning component of the supervision cycle can take a variety of different forms. Although schoolwide training and professional development are often considered the primary mechanisms to support professional learning in schools, we advocate for multiple differentiated forms of support for teacher learning (Bredeson, 2003; Knight, 2008). Many leaders may want to design a professional development workshop for all teachers to kick off work on the science practices, but it is important to think of multiple, differentiated ways to support ongoing development. This can include accessing online resources, establishing routines for peer coaching, and creating collaborative planning opportunities for teachers to work together on implementing practices. In Chapter 6, we share our approach to professional learning and describe the tools we have developed to support teacher and leader learning about the science practices.

Crafting a Schoolwide Approach

The supervision cycle requires careful planning and preparation. Given the importance of preparing for an iterative process that provides multiple opportunities for growth, instructional leaders need to engage in a preliminary planning process that addresses the nuts and bolts of implementing a targeted supervision cycle. We suggest that instructional leaders, in conversation with district science specialists and teachers, identify a particular set of science practices to focus on in a given year. For example, a school may decide to hone teachers' capabilities to enact the investigating practices. Once a focus has been defined, leaders can engage in three steps of planning that include assessing existing resources, scheduling each step of the cycle, and differentiating science supervision for (i.e., knowing the different profiles of) all teachers involved. By proactively mapping out an approach to science supervision, leaders can maximize the potential of engaging in this endeavor and ensure they maintain a focus on the process.

Assess Existing Resources

Prior to engaging in the supervision cycle, it is important to analyze the lay of the land in terms of existing resources that can support the process. Often, the district's central office may include science specialists or coaches with focused expertise in the science practices. Existing routines can support professional learning, such as grade-level meetings or common planning time. Relationships among teachers can also serve as a resource for collaborative learning opportunities. Anchoring the supervision cycle on a shared set of tools, such as those offered in this book, can provide a common language that guides conversations for each step of the supervision cycle. It's important to approach these resources with a schoolwide plan. How can instructional leadership leverage these resources to establish a coherent and coordinated plan for implementing a supervision cycle in science?

Schedule Each Step of the Supervision Cycle

Often, instructional leaders find scheduling the biggest barrier to overcome when implementing a meaningful supervision cycle. Although it is not always possible to schedule everything in advance, it is helpful to map out a tentative plan for each step of the cycle that builds in school-wide supervision. Although instructional leaders often set aside time for classroom observation, it is crucial to incorporate time for feedback sessions soon after those observations and establish an expectation for follow-up meetings at the outset. Although professional learning opportunities may not always occur as formal, planned training sessions, some professional learning opportunities can be determined and scheduled in advance, such as devoting a half day of professional development to focused discussion of how to integrate a particular science practice into the current unit teachers are preparing.

Disruptions to the plan are inevitable, but crafting a schedule that aligns with the school calendar in advance can help instructional leaders commit to engaging in the cycle. This also sets the stage for a coordinated effort to supervise science for all teachers—not just a few. How can instructional leaders establish a routine, staged schedule that will ensure all teachers have opportunities to be observed, receive feedback, and engage in professional learning?

Differentiate Science Supervision for All Teachers

Before embarking on the supervision cycle, instructional leaders need to take time to consider the kinds of support teachers will need to develop new instructional techniques. Differentiating the supervision cycle to account for teachers at various stages of their career, with different levels of expertise, and with different motivations to learn new skills will help make the process as effective as possible.

In her book *Never Underestimate Your Teachers*, Robyn Jackson (2013) explains that teachers can be categorized within one of four quadrants based on their motivation, or will, to engage in improvement, and their capabilities, or skill, at instruction. Some "high-skill, high-will" teachers are extremely proficient at instruction and interested in engaging in ongoing improvement. Other "high-skill, low-will" teachers may be highly skilled but feel they have learned all they need to know and are thus hesitant, or even resistant, to learning new instructional approaches. Some "low-skill, low-will" teachers may struggle in the classroom but are resistant to improvement efforts. Others lack proficiency either because they are novices or because they have not had supportive opportunities to learn but are categorized as "low-skill, high-will" teachers because they are eager professional learners.

Although the skill/will matrix is widely used as a tool to support supervision in general, we want to emphasize that teachers fall in different quadrants for different subjects. Even if they are responsible for teaching across subject areas, most teachers have a subject in which they feel most comfortable or have committed the most effort to improving. Often, these subjects are English language arts and math, which are also frequently the focus of professional development. For this reason, a teacher may be high skill/high will in these subjects but low skill in science. It is also important to figure out who is motivated to learn more about science and who may be less committed. Some teachers, just like some leaders, may not understand the urgency to focus on science, a subject that has often been marginalized in the accountability system.

Ultimately, differentiating science supervision requires you to determine where teachers fall on the skill/will matrix, specific to science. For those with high will and low skill, hands-on, consistent, frequent observation and feedback can be paired with both formal and informal learning opportunities, such as professional development and visits to colleagues' classrooms. By contrast, those with low will and high skill might become increasingly resistant if observations are too frequent. However, their will might increase if they are incorporated into the cycle as mentors or models for those with lower skill. Depending on their engagement in the supervision cycle, those with both low skill and low will need hands-on support from instructional leaders who will also need to find ways to motivate them to engage in learning.

Leverage Goal Setting for Science Supervision

Many schools have implemented a goal-setting process that is linked to a formal evaluation system (Marshall, 2013). For example, many educators are required to establish and track a set of SMART (specific, measurable, action-oriented, realistic, and timed) goals. These goals are related to both student learning and professional practice. As they engage in goal setting with teachers, instructional leaders encourage them to identify both individual and team goals that stem from the supervision cycle. This provides structure to their improvement efforts over the course of the year. Though these goals are often developed individually between a teacher and his or her supervisor, some instructional leaders have found ways to craft coherence and consistency by establishing specific schoolwide goals and encouraging teachers to tie their individual goals to those. By contrast, when teachers have the ability to craft team or partner goals, they can collaborate, reflect together, and work toward a common outcome.

Often, both schoolwide and individual goals are grounded in the accountability system, which privileges test scores in language arts and mathematics. As a result, these goals are often oriented to those subjects rather than tied to initiatives in other subjects. However, if you want to emphasize science reform and implement the science practices, we recommend you anchor the goal-setting process in science. For example, you can establish SMART goals aligned with integrating science practices in the classroom. Setting schoolwide goals for science improvements and linking individual SMART goals to the implementation of the science practices can help leaders and teachers formalize their commitment to science reform and create schoolwide accountability for engaging in the supervision cycle with a focus on science.

Taking the time to prepare allows instructional leaders to map out a supervision cycle that takes advantage of available resources, aligns with the school calendar, and leverages the will and skill of teachers. Preparing to engage in a schoolwide effort to implement the science practices will ensure meaningful engagement in the supervision cycle.

A Few Practical Tips

Build Trust over Time

Instructional leaders typically work closely with teachers to develop trusting relationships—with the goal of fostering support and growth rather than enforcement and accountability—and successful supervision is modeled after the teacher-student relationship instead of the employer-employee relationship. It takes time to build trust, so keep in mind that for the first few rotations of the supervision cycle, that should be the primary goal. Maintain a shared focus on the science practices and tools so the conversation does not feel too personal. Build a connection to and confidence in the process by starting small and with constant encouragement.

Two effective strategies—when working with teachers and principals—are admitting vulnerability and giving permission for mistakes. Demonstrating vulnerability might mean confiding in the teachers you lead about your personal struggles with the content and talking about the times the work was hard for you. Maybe it took you a long time to fully understand a particular science practice, or maybe you needed to watch a video multiple times to decipher the standards. It is amazing how relieved teachers look after sharing such anecdotes. Teachers and principals are more open and trusting when they see the leader as a learner just like them!

Giving permission for mistakes works in a similar way. Learners need to know it's OK if they don't understand everything right away and it's OK to experiment with new strategies. Explicit permission from an expert or leader to make mistakes or go slowly helps everyone feel less pressure and be more open to trying new things. For example, if a teacher asks if he can just focus on getting kids to talk more to one another—rather than take on the entire practice of argumentation—he needs the affirmation that this is a perfect first step toward argumentation because student-to-student discourse is at the heart of that practice. If he spent time working on student talk, then the rest would be much easier. Not only did this help the teacher feel more comfortable, but it also developed trust with the instructional leader because it became obvious they were thinking alike.

Foster Collaboration Among Teachers

Instructional leaders should partner with teachers, and teachers should partner with one another to develop expertise as a community. The supervision cycle presents opportunities for teachers to learn together through professional development. Such opportunities aim to build shared knowledge and reward growth across the school. As leaders learn more about teachers' relative strengths, they can strategically pair teachers together and create professional learning that brings them together. Structuring collaboration through shared planning time, peer observation, and professional development will help create more meaningful engagement and growth through the supervision cycle.

Choice is also an important aspect of effective collaboration for teachers (and students). Teachers are more likely to buy into trying new things when they can choose who they work with, what they want to focus on, and how long they have to collaborate. So what does this look like? It really depends on your school and district culture. However, here are a few structures that we have seen work at schools:

- Teachers self-select partners and craft a plan for professional learning using provided resources, such as the ILSP website. Teachers then submit their plan to their supervisor for feedback.
- Teachers meet regularly with their grade-level colleagues and select from a menu of professional development options created by the principal. This menu contains a variety of choices, such as observing a colleague (and using the continuum), reflecting on a video together, or inviting a curriculum coordinator to observe them teach.
- The principal provides regular opportunities for the entire staff to work in small groups on a common activity, such as analyzing a transcript of a science lesson. Teachers are given the option to meet at other times to further explore the ideas generated during these meetings.

Maintain Transparency About the Supervision Cycle

As instructional leaders engage in the supervision cycle, they should make their approach, the tools they plan to use, and the steps of the process as visible and explicit to teachers as they can. By working from a shared set of tools, teachers will have a clear set of expectations. A teacher once remarked to us that simply having a copy of the Science Practices Continuum on hand was enough to prompt her to reevaluate her instruction: "I was probably going toward a Level 1, but I stopped and changed what students were doing to be more in line with Level 3." This recognition allowed for a discussion of other situations in which the teacher could deepen her instruction of the science practices.

Transparency also builds trust by ensuring that teachers are not surprised by what's coming. Therefore, we recommend leaders share their plans for structuring feedback that highlights a neutral approach focused on instruction rather than individuals. Ultimately, educating teachers about the supervision cycle provides opportunities to discuss the most effective ways to structure the process and allows leaders to learn and adjust as they engage in the cycle.

Returning to Principal Thompson

In her office later that day, Principal Thompson and Ms. Martinelli talk about how the class went. They take out the continuum and look together at the investigating practice.

Principal Thompson notes, "It seemed like you set up the procedures for them, and they were able to follow them." Ms. Martinelli says she felt like she had succeeded in setting up an investigation, but she still does not know how to get students to decide on some aspect of it. Principal Thompson points out that a 3rd grade teacher has been working on this, so perhaps Ms. Martinelli could set up time to visit her class next week and see how she encourages students to design their own investigations.

She explains, "Then we can check back in about this aspect of the practice when I visit your class next month." As they end the meeting, Principal Thompson reminds Ms. Martinelli that this is new for everyone and that they will keep learning together as they work on their goal of integrating the science practices.

Discussion Questions
Reflection

1. What ideas from this chapter resonated with your own experiences of supervision? What ideas were different from what you have experienced?

2. What do you think Principal Thompson should encourage Ms. Martinelli to do during the next rotation? What might you encourage Ms. Martinelli to do the same and/or differently?

Application

1. Which parts of the supervision cycle are already in place at your school? Are the parts coordinated with one another?
2. In your current school context:
   — What resources would you want to leverage to establish a supervision cycle focused on the science practices?
   — How would you approach scheduling?
   — How might you differentiate support for teachers in different quadrants of the skill/will matrix?
3. What challenges might you face as you implement the supervision cycle in your context?

4

Observation

Mr. Taylor is a school principal who will observe Ms. Anderson's class today. He is excited for this observation because Ms. Anderson is one of the school's strongest teachers, and her students are consistently engaged and motivated. Today, Ms. Anderson is doing an introduction to a unit on the moon. When Mr. Taylor enters the classroom, students have just finished watching a video about the moon and Ms. Anderson is asking, "What did you learn about the moon from the video?"

One student raises his hand and says, "The moon has craters on it." Ms. Anderson responds, "What a great observation! Let's all write this down in our space journal." She then writes the observation on the whiteboard as every student copies it down into their journals. After a few students share their observations, Ms. Anderson asks, "Do we know if the moon makes its own light?" Nobody answers the question, and after 15 seconds of wait time, Ms. Anderson says, "Help me finish this sentence: The moon reflects light like a..." Students still do not answer her question, so after another 10 seconds of wait time, Ms. Anderson completes her own sentence, saying, "The moon reflects light like a mirror. Let's say *reflect* together!" All students then repeat the word *reflect* in unison and mime a hand motion that represents holding a mirror.

After this discussion, Mr. Taylor leaves Ms. Anderson's class impressed by what he saw. All the students were on task and engaged the entire time; tracked the speaker; contributed ideas; and practiced their listening, speaking, and writing skills. In addition, Ms. Anderson developed her students' vocabulary using spoken and kinesthetic ways of learning. It seems like Ms. Anderson hit all the marks, but given his unfamiliarity with the subject, Mr. Taylor admits he is unsure what science at this age is supposed to look like.

Theorizing Observation: The Importance of Noticing

Mr. Taylor noticed a lot of important content-neutral features of Ms. Anderson's classroom, including her students' engagement, the range of voices in the classroom, and her approach to vocabulary instruction. These are all important components of strong instruction, but by themselves they do not advance students' science skills and understandings as envisioned by the NGSS. Given that Mr. Taylor, like most principals, does not have a background in science, it makes sense that he would more easily see these general pedagogical features of a classroom. Unfortunately, that focus limits his ability to support Ms. Anderson as she pushes her students to engage in the type of scientific thinking expected by the NGSS. To support this work, Mr. Taylor needs an understanding of the science practices and what they look like along a continuum of complexity (see Chapter 2). In addition, he also needs more experience recognizing these practices when he observes classroom instruction.

In this chapter, we discuss strategies for observation that can help instructional leaders such as Mr. Taylor support instruction of the science practices. We believe the foundation to this work is noticing when teachers engage their students in authentic practices of science. Therefore, we begin this chapter with an explanation of what we mean by *noticing* and then share tools to help you notice when teachers engage students in the science practices.

In recent years, observation has become an increasingly important responsibility for instructional leaders tasked with improving teacher quality. New teacher evaluations and schoolwide supervision systems rely on frequent and ongoing observations carried out by supervisors who may or may not have content expertise in the subjects they observe (Donaldson, 2009; Lowenhaupt & McNeill, 2019). To support this emphasis on observation, various tools and resources have been developed, such as instructional rubrics (e.g., Danielson, 2007), online software to facilitate documentation, and general guidance on the process (e.g., Marshall, 2013).

These have all provided important scaffolding to supervisors, but they tend to present a content-neutral view of instruction, emphasizing general pedagogical features such as student engagement or the use of objectives. However, we know there are significant subject-specific differences in what constitutes "good instruction" (Nelson & Sassi, 2005). Strategies to promote literacy may not be the best strategies to use when teaching a new math concept, and what might on the surface look like student engagement in a science classroom may not be the kind of active involvement some science lessons require. For this reason, supervisors need help recognizing these subject differences and understanding how these distinctions inform the supervision process.

We find it helpful to use the idea of noticing when thinking about supporting subject-specific supervision. Classrooms are complex and busy places; it is impossible to observe every aspect of instruction happening at any given point in time. Instead, and based on their own focus and interests, observers tend to focus on specific aspects that are of interest to themselves personally. During observation, the act of noticing refers to the act of focusing on specific things we are drawn to and how we make meaning of them (Sherin & van Es, 2005).

We can train ourselves to get better at noticing various aspects of instruction. One way to do this is to learn about a specific feature of instruction and exclusively attend to that during an observation. Another way is to use a tool, such as a rubric or checklist, that anchors the observation and frames how and what we purposefully document. In the next section, we discuss some of the tools we have developed and their intended uses.

Using the Observation Tools

The steps included in this section use the Science Practices Continuum and the Science Instruction Observation Form (see Appendix B; also www.sciencepracticesleadership.com/supervision-tools.html) to focus your observation on the science practices.

Prepare for the Observation

Refer to the continuum. In Chapter 2, we introduced the Science Practices Continuum, a tool designed to serve as a scaffold for instructional leaders as they work to support the science practices. The continuum provides specific explanations of what the practices might look like at varying levels of proficiency. As we discussed, the two versions of the continuum can either train your eye toward students or teachers. The continuum also reminds us of key ideas about science instruction that go hand in hand with the science practices, which, in turn, inform our observations of science instruction. As you prepare for an observation, you may want to revisit the continuum. We suggest printing a copy to have in hand as you enter the classroom. This can anchor your observations and help you notice the practices themselves.

Decide on a focus. It is important to keep in mind how you plan to narrow your focus during an observation. Perhaps you have been working on a particular practice with your teachers, or maybe you had a chance to meet with the teacher ahead of time to decide on a focal practice. By contrast, you might be conducting an informal, unplanned observation and therefore must wait and see what is happening in the classroom after you enter it. Regardless of the nature of your observation, it is important to be clear about your purpose before you set foot in the classroom. We recommend identifying one or two science practices on which to focus. Even though teachers may be integrating more than two practices in a particular lesson, we have found that observers often have a hard time making sense of more than two at a time. If you do not have an opportunity to identify practices in advance, you can decide to focus on the two most prevalent practices that emerge during instruction.

Let's say you are going to observe a lesson that involves an experiment. The teacher has been purposefully trying to target the science practice of Planning and Carrying Out Investigations. Before you go into the classroom, you decide that you will observe for this practice as your primary focus. You review the continuum and remind yourself of specific things to look for with this practice. For example, are students simply following a recipe of steps, or do they design some aspect of the investigation? What kinds of insights do students get to share as they set up the investigation? What choices do they have as they run the investigation?

You also revisit the other practices in case a second focal practice emerges during your observation. Consequently, you decide to pay careful attention to the associated science practices of Asking Questions and Using Mathematics and Computational Thinking because you realize they are important in the context of a lesson focused on investigating. You will likely notice other aspects of instruction, such as whether students are paying attention and how long it takes the teacher to set up the experiment, but you have prepared yourself to notice instruction in a particular way, honing in on the science practices as you observe.

Use the Observation Form

How you document your observation shapes what you notice, just like a camera lens shapes a photograph. To help maintain a focus on the science practices, the Science Instruction Observation Form (see Appendix B) provides a structure for documenting what an observer notices. At the same time, the design of the form allows room for jotting down additional notes and insights, helping the observer keep track of the complex set of practices in a science classroom.

A key feature of the form is that it asks you to select one or two practices as a focus for your observation. As discussed, you may have already identified a focal practice before entering the classroom. The observation form includes space for two but includes the names of all the practices as a reference. We encourage you to keep all the science practices in mind as you identify the two that are central to the observed lesson.

The form is purposefully open-ended, encouraging observations in as much detail as possible. The goal here is to gather evidence about the focal practices so the observer can justify the ratings identified at the bottom of the form. These ratings are intended to align with the Science Practices Continuum, which you should plan to have on hand. Some instructional leaders find it helpful to have paper copies of both the continuum and the observation form to help them stay focused, notice features of instruction that are relevant to particular practices, and identify where on the continuum a given lesson may fall. Other instructional leaders fill in the observation form during the lesson; after the observation, they return to the continuum and use the gathered evidence to explain a rationale for their ratings.

In doing this work, it is helpful to keep in mind the three instructional elements that support student engagement in all the science practices: grounded in explaining natural phenomena, focused on building and critiquing ideas using evidence, and student-directed and collaborative. These features can help support more equitable science classrooms in which students use their shared experience around a phenomenon to collaboratively build their science understandings. This focus on the science practices can help create opportunities in which each student is known, heard, and supported.

Practice Using the Tools

Now that you have had a chance to learn about the observation tools, let's try our hand at using them in the classroom. The following vignette comes from Mr. Rodgers's 5th grade classroom. The class is learning about chemical reactions as part of a unit on the structure and properties of matter, and they have been keeping a chart of the investigations they have been doing, classifying each reaction as a chemical reaction or not. Before beginning the next investigation, Mr. Rodgers wants to review what they have learned so far.

As you read through the vignette, refer to the continuum and jot down notes on the observation form. Here are some guiding questions to keep in mind as you read:

- What science practices do you notice in Mr. Rodgers's lessons?
- What evidence is present that Mr. Rodgers engaged students thoughtfully in those practices?
- Where on the continuum does the lesson fall?
- How could the lesson be improved to move it further along the continuum?

Mr. Rodgers: Let's take out our charts and use our data to remind ourselves about chemical reactions. Adam?

Adam: In a chemical reaction, new materials are made. Like when we did the experiment yesterday with the baking soda, sugar, road salt, and that red liquid. When they all mixed, it made a gas. We didn't have a gas before we started.

Lila: That was cool. The plastic baggie got big. I thought it might explode. But I have a question. How do we know we didn't have something that was the gas, but it was just a liquid or a solid before?

Drew: I'm confused. If we put two things together and they make a gas, then we made something new?

Lila: Probably, but remember the experiment we did with boiling water? The water turned into water vapor, which is a gas, but it's still H_2O. It's not new stuff.

Adam: Well, the bag also got hot. That is also a sign of a chemical reaction.

The class continues to discuss their observations. Then Mr. Rodgers tells students that they will be repeating the experiment with the salt, sugar, baking soda, and red liquid (phenol red). However, instead of just putting the materials together in a bag to see what happens, they will be experimenting to figure out what combination of three substances actually causes the chemical reaction. He asks students to work together in groups to plan how to conduct the investigation and create a data table where they can record their observations. Mr. Rodgers listens in as one group discusses the table.

Amelia: OK, we need to plan how we will do this investigation.

Ethan: We can only change one thing at a time so let's write down all the different combinations we should try.

The students make a list of all the different combinations, making sure they only change one substance at a time.

Amelia: Now we can make the data table.

Jeff: I will write down which three substances we are trying. We need to make a space to write down what happens, too, right?

Ethan: You mean, how will we know if a chemical reaction happened?

Amelia: The stuff in the bag will bubble.

Ethan: So maybe the second column could be yes or no, whether there are bubbles or not.

Amelia: What about the temperature? That will change if there is a chemical reaction.

The students continue their work. After the groups have time to discuss their investigations and data tables, Mr. Rodgers calls the class back together.

Mr. Rodgers: I'm seeing different types of data tables you are using. Let's put up a few of them around the room and see how they compare. I'm going to give you sticky notes to write questions for the students who designed the data tables. It's important that if you write a question, it's one that asks about a specific part of the data table or about something you do not understand. For example, I might ask Amelia, Jeff, and Ethan why their data table has a column for *yes* or *no*. Yes or no for what?

The students move in small groups around the room. Using sticky notes, they ask questions about the data tables. After, Mr. Rodgers gives the groups time to read the questions and make changes to their tables. The students then collect their data.

In the next class, students conduct their experiments. The day after, Mr. Rodgers starts class by having students take out their data tables and talk within their groups about what they learned from the experiment.

Amanda: We saw that when the baking soda, salt, and red liquid were mixed, a chemical reaction happened.

Eliza: Well, we saw that there were bubbles. So that means a chemical reaction happened.

Amanda: Right. That was the combination that made something new, which was the gas. The bag got hot too.

Justin: So what about the sugar? I mean, it turned into something red when we added the red liquid.

Eliza: I don't think that's a chemical reaction. It just changed colors.

Justin: Oh, I get it. It's like the melting ice. It turns into water, but it is still the same stuff: H_2O.

Mr. Rodgers explains that each student should write a scientific explanation to answer the following question: What three substances caused the chemical reaction? He shows students a graphic organizer that has three parts: claim, evidence, and reasoning.

Mr. Rodgers: Can someone remind me what a claim is?

Justin: The answer to the science question we asked.

Mr. Rodgers: Right. The first thing you will do is write a sentence that answers our question: What three substances cause the chemical reaction?

Eliza: And then we use our data tables for the next part?

Mr. Rodgers: Right. Your data become your evidence when you use it to explain your claim. But remember, we are not going to just copy our data tables in there. We are going to write down in sentences the data that make sense to include.

Amanda: So maybe not everything we tried?

Mr. Rodgers: Probably not. But you will have to decide what to include.

Ethan: Oh, I remember the last part: the reasoning. That's the science idea.

Jeff: For this one, what would we write? What a chemical reaction is?

Mr. Rodgers: You are going to have to make that decision, but don't forget that the science idea should show why your evidence explains the claim. Why does the data you used help explain your answer to the question? Remember, scientific explanations always explain how or why something happens. Today, you will have a chance to do your writing. Tomorrow, we will have some time to read one another's answers to help make everyone's explanations even better.

Take another look at your notes on the continuum and observation form. In this vignette, we found the strongest evidence for three science practices: Planning and Carrying Out Investigations, Analyzing and Interpreting Data, and Constructing Explanations.

Mr. Rodgers's students had already conducted a variation of this experiment (with a plastic baggie), so they were familiar with the materials. However, Mr. Rodgers asked them to design an investigation to determine which three ingredients would cause a chemical reaction. He could have easily given students a procedure, but by asking them to do it themselves, he provided students with an opportunity to make meaningful decisions about what they would do.

At the same time, however, he knew that students might not be able to do this design work on their own, which is why he waited until they were familiar with the system to work on the design. In addition, he asked students to give feedback on their investigations so they could make use of one another's expertise. For example, Amelia suggested they look for a temperature change when combining things, which is an idea that Ethan may not have come up with on his own.

One place we might push Mr. Rodgers is in establishing a joint goal for the investigation in the first place. Here, Mr. Rodgers simply told the class they would be looking for a combination of three ingredients that causes a reaction, but he could have facilitated a brief class discussion to draw out that question from students. This would have allowed students to make more complex decisions about the various components of the investigation and deepened their thinking about its design.

We also see multiple opportunities for students to analyze and interpret data in this vignette. Because Mr. Rodgers has students performing several investigations with the same materials and consistently refers to the main goal of identifying chemical reactions, his students are able to develop their understanding of what observations indicate the presence of a chemical reaction. This is more effective than simply telling students how to tell if a reaction occurs; students are forced to construct the ideas themselves and defend them with their own observations.

For example, Lila and Justin both refer to previous experiences of water boiling to make sense of what they saw in the investigations and whether that phenomenon counts as a chemical reaction. In addition, we saw that Mr. Rodgers gave his students multiple opportunities to make decisions about which data to collect, as evidenced by allowing them to construct their own tables with support from him and their peers. Mr. Rodgers told students to use a data table, but he could have allowed students to discuss that decision. We do not believe that was necessary in this case, given the large number of other cognitively demanding decisions he asked his students to make.

Finally, we see in this lesson students engaged in constructing scientific explanations. Mr. Rodgers's use of a claim-evidence-reasoning framework provides students with a scaffold for constructing their explanations, and he spends time clarifying the definitions of each part and what constitutes an appropriate claim or effective evidence. In addition, Mr. Rodgers makes clear that the purpose of a scientific explanation is to explain how or why something happens—rather than to simply describe a natural phenomenon.

That being said, we were unsure if the guiding question (Which three substances cause a chemical reaction?) really pushes students to use *how* or *why* thinking in their explanations. We need more evidence from students' explanations to fully see how well they were engaging in this practice. Nevertheless, the structures and directions Mr. Rodgers used allow students to think deeply about what happens in their chemical reaction investigations—and why it happens—rather than simply recounting a hands-on experience.

Figure 4.1 summarizes what we noticed from the vignette and is written as if we observed the classes in real time. Also included are our thoughts on where we might place this instruction on the continuum for each practice we noticed, along with our rationale for those levels. We encourage you to compare your form with ours to see if what you noticed aligns with what we noticed.

We know there are benefits and constraints of practicing with written resources such as this vignette. When you are just starting to notice these practices, it can be easier to find them in written words you can reread and analyze at your own pace. Unfortunately, real-life observations will not be as easy as this. Therefore, we encourage you to continue practicing your noticing as you head into classrooms.

If you would like more resources, check out the videos we have on our website at www.sciencepracticesleadership.com. These examples allow you to watch real classroom interactions with an eye toward science practices. We have also included observation forms filled out with our thoughts for each video to help you hone your own observations.

A Few Practical Tips
Form a Perspective of Understanding

In the context of reform, teachers are asked to change their daily practice in a myriad of ways, especially at the K–8 level where teachers are responsible for multiple subject areas—all of which are constantly evolving. All too often, the expectations are unclear, and curriculum standards and documents are overwhelming. Recognizing that administrators and teachers are partners in improving classroom instruction requires everyone to bring a perspective of understanding to the work.

Change takes time, trust, and patience. Integrating the science practices is no easy task. During observation, as well as in other aspects of the supervision cycle, it is important for observers to approach the classroom from a place of understanding. It is all too easy to be overly critical of what others are doing, particularly when student learning is at stake.

FIGURE 4.1 : Mr. Rodgers's Science Instruction Observation Form

Science Instruction Observation Form

Educator Name: Supervisor Name:

Observation Date: Observation Time/Duration:

Intended Observation Focus:

NGSS Practices		
Which practices are observed?		
Investigation Practices	*Sensemaking Practices*	*Critiquing Practices*
☐ 1. Asking Questions	☐ 2. Developing and Using Models	☐ 7. Engaging in Argument from Evidence
☑ 3. Planning and Carrying Out Investigations	☑ 4. Analyzing and Interpreting Data	☐ 8. Obtaining, Evaluating, and Communicating Information
☐ 5. Using Mathematics and Computational Thinking	☑ 6. Constructing Explanations	

Observation Evidence
What are the educator and students saying and doing?

Part I

- Begins with review of what students have learned so far about chemical reactions
  - Multiple students speaking
  - Students express confusion but teacher does not immediately give answer

- Student design follow-up to yesterday's experiment
  - Question: What combination of substances actually causes the chemical reaction?
  - Students work in groups to plan investigation and data table

- Gallery walk of data tables
  - Students compare data tables across groups
  - Use sticky notes to ask one another questions
  - Have time to modify data tables based on peer feedback

Part 2

- Students discuss experiment results in groups
  - Students think about what counts as a chemical reaction
  - Comparing to experiences with melting ice

- Teacher reviews components of scientific explanation and then students write an explanation

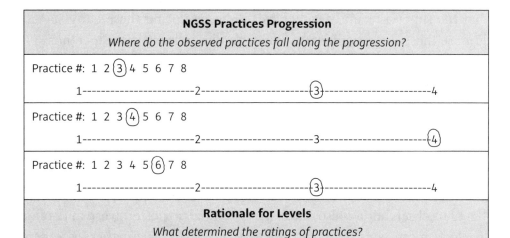

NGSS Practices Progression

Where do the observed practices fall along the progression?

Practice #:　1　2　③　4　5　6　7　8

1-----------------------2-----------------------③-----------------------4

Practice #:　1　2　3　④　5　6　7　8

1-----------------------2-----------------------3-----------------------④

Practice #:　1　2　3　4　5　⑥　7　8

1-----------------------2-----------------------③-----------------------4

Rationale for Levels

What determined the ratings of practices?

Practice 3: Students were designing investigations with support from the teacher and peers. They made decisions about what controls to use, but the teacher already told them the goal was to combine three substances at a time. What if the students had a conversation first about how to determine which component(s) were causing the reaction?

Practice 4: Students were organizing data into a table and used past experiences with boiling water to find patterns in the data they found. The teacher told them to use a table, but students determined how to construct the table using feedback from the teacher or peers, forcing them to make decisions about what is important for analyzing the data from the investigation.

Practice 6: Students were asked to make a claim to answer what three substances make the chemical reaction happen. The teacher encouraged students to describe how or why the phenomenon was happening, but it was unclear how well the descriptive question (What three substances cause a chemical reaction to occur?) might support that. More evidence is needed from the students' actual explanations to know how well they engage in this practice.

However, the best way to shift daily practice is to do so incrementally and over time. Focusing on the science practices provides a concrete, tangible emphasis for observation. Try to keep your attention (and critique) directly on the practices, and remember that you are all learning these practices together.

One additional caveat: When supervisors and teachers are both in the early stages of learning about these resources and strategies, there is an inherent tension. After all, if supervisors are still learning, there's a natural skepticism that they are unable to evaluate teachers' instruction fairly. It is therefore important to acknowledge this tension and use the continuum to ground conversations. It is also important to understand that the supervisor and teacher can disagree during these early stages. Just use those disagreements as opportunities to learn more together.

Establish Observation Routines

Changing daily practice isn't easy and doesn't happen overnight. We have found that regular, consistent observations—coupled with immediate, bite-sized feedback—can support teachers best as they adapt to their practice. Frequent visits also ensure that leaders understand the scope of the class and can place their observations in the appropriate context. Regular observations also have the potential to foster trust and offer teachers more consistent and relevant support. By creating an observation routine, supervisors create a culture of ongoing learning and growth. Acknowledging the constraints of many supervisors' schedules, we recommend shorter, more frequent visits (10–15 minutes), which are more powerful than less frequent, longer visits. It's also important to establish that these observations do not become part of any official evaluation documents. If they must be part of an evaluation cycle, make sure to reiterate that the focus is on growth, not any type of "score" on the continuum.

Engage in Supervision Collaboratively

Learning new strategies for the classroom can be daunting, yet it can also be exciting if you're part of a group working collaboratively to puzzle through the best way to make the strategies most effective—and the learning most meaningful. Sharing protocols and processes, administrators and teachers can work together in an open conversation about how best to integrate the practices. Providing access to the tools in advance of observations, discussing examples of the practices together, and helping teachers identify focal practices for observation can help create transparency in the process.

Teachers may even want to use the continuum and observation form for their own peer observations. As they learn to use the tools and interpret the results, you may find yourself discussing with them where they might place themselves on the continuum. Remember, as you engage in observation, the goal should be maintaining as transparent a process as possible to minimize surprises and build trust.

Returning to Mr. Taylor

As he writes up his notes from his observation of Ms. Anderson's class, Mr. Taylor remembers the Science Practices Continuum. He realizes that tool might help him resolve his questions about whether the class he had observed was as effective as he originally thought. After reviewing the continuum, he realizes there were all sorts of classroom interactions he had not thought to look for when watching Ms. Anderson's science lesson. He realizes his notes do not reflect the degree to which students investigated the natural world, made sense of evidence from those investigations, or tried to explain how or why a phenomenon took place. Suddenly, he is much less confident about his observations than when he walked out of the classroom.

Based on these new thoughts, Mr. Taylor decides he should go back into Ms. Anderson's classroom and conduct a more focused observation of another science lesson. He reviews the continuum again and decides he is most interested in seeing how students analyze data and create explanations; those practices seem most aligned with the work the school is doing around claims and evidence in other subject areas so he is curious to see how they may look in science. He prints out a copy of the Science Practices Observation Form and completes it with the two focal practices to make sure he stays focused on them. He then makes a note to ask Ms. Anderson when he can come in again to practice his observation skills.

With these new tools, Mr. Taylor feels excited about starting to work with Ms. Anderson on these science practices

Discussion Questions

Reflection

1. What are two takeaways for you from this chapter?
2. Think of a time you were observed while teaching. How much did the observer focus on general pedagogy versus concerns specific to

your discipline? What do you wish the observer had noticed that was missed?

3. How much do you tend to notice content-neutral or science-specific facets of instruction when you are observing classrooms?

4. What is the value of training yourself to observe science lessons with a more science-specific lens?

Application

1. How will you use the tools in this chapter to improve science instruction at your school?

2. What can you do to train yourself to notice more science-specific facets of instruction when you observe?

3. Who can you enlist as collaborators to help develop your ability to observe science lessons in your school?

4. It can be overwhelming to try to develop your ability to notice all the practices at the same time. Which one or two science practices most speak to you or do you find easiest to notice? How will you work to notice those practices more consistently in your next few observations?

5

Feedback

Dr. Dean enters Mr. Stuart's 1st grade classroom, looking forward to observing a science lesson. Mr. Stuart is a new teacher but has already developed a reputation in the school for doing lots of interesting science activities in his classroom. As Dr. Dean settles down in a seat near students, she watches Mr. Stuart introduce a new unit and then show a short video of animals in the wild. The students are visibly excited as they watch, and hands go up immediately. Mr. Stuart calls on a few students who share their experiences with pets at home or observations of wild animals outside.

One student says, "I wonder why squirrels have such long, fluffy tails." Mr. Stuart responds that this is a great question because the class is going to be learning about the different parts of animals and their jobs in helping animals get what they need to live.

He says, "We call these different parts *structures* and the jobs they do for the animal *functions*." Mr. Stuart then asks what other questions the students have about animal structures and functions. As students call out questions, Mr. Stuart records them on chart paper. "Wow," he says. "You have a lot of questions. This is what scientists do; they ask questions." Mr. Stuart tells students that as scientists, they will try to answer these questions as they learn more.

Dr. Dean leaves the room, impressed at how enthusiastic the students were and how many questions they were able to generate. She also appreciates that Mr. Stuart had students do the asking, since in many classrooms, she sees the teacher pose most of the questions. However, as a principal who has been using the Science Practices Continuum to supervise teachers, she recognizes that despite the students' engagement and excitement, this instruction is at a Level 2 for the practice of Asking Questions. Her rationale is that Mr. Stuart did not explain that scientific questions are those that are answerable with data, and he did not support students to ask these types of questions. Dr. Dean considers what type of feedback could help Mr. Stuart move forward on the continuum, where students would be more authentically engaged in this practice.

Theorizing Feedback: The Role of Feedback in Instructional Growth

Providing meaningful feedback to teachers is one of the most challenging—yet essential—parts of the supervision cycle. Feedback is one of the key ways that teachers understand how to improve their practice and their students' learning. Feedback that accomplishes this goal offers teachers concrete "bite-sized" strategies they can readily employ in their classrooms (Bambrick-Santoyo, 2012). Research has confirmed that when post-observation feedback is specific and meaningful, teachers' instruction can improve (Myung & Martinez, 2013). This feedback, however, is rarely effective when simply stated to teachers. Rather, the feedback needs to be provided as part of a well-planned post-observation conference.

In this chapter, we discuss strategies for providing feedback that can push your teachers' instruction forward on the continuum. We present a tool you can use to plan and implement post-observation conferences with teachers and a resource of specific instructional strategies for each science practice.

The post-observation conference is an important opportunity for teachers to talk about the instruction that was observed and for the observer to ask questions about student learning and the teacher's instructional decisions. The inclusion of observed areas of strength in the lesson is key to reducing anxiety for the teacher and creating a space for more critical feedback later (Myung & Martinez, 2013). When specific ideas are offered or discussed to improve the teacher's instruction, it is important that they consist of small, actionable, mutually agreed-upon recommendations that are directly related to a specific instructional or student learning goal (Wiggins, 2012). For teachers to improve student participation in the science practices, the feedback must be directly connected to these practices.

Using the Feedback Tools

We developed two tools to support you in conducting post-observation conferences anchored in the science practices. The first is the Post-Observation Conference Worksheet. This tool is aimed at helping you plan post-observation conferences and document the discussions that occur there. The Instructional Strategies Tool is a series of instructional recommendations for each science practice. These are useful when teachers need concrete ideas to try to improve their instruction of a specific science practice.

Use the Post-Observation Conference Worksheet

The Post-Observation Conference Worksheet (see Appendix B) is designed to align with the research-based features of post-observation conferences. The goal is to help you plan ways to support teachers in continually improving their instruction of the science practices. The Worksheet consists of five categories: praise, focal science practices, probing questions, key levers, and future plans.

Praise. Start your conference by mentioning something specific from your observation that was positive. If possible, reference an area in which the teacher demonstrated growth from your last observation.

If not, identify a new strength. This sets the tone for the conference and lets teachers know that you noticed strengths in their instruction.

Focal science practices. Next, identify the one science practice you will focus on during this post-observation conference. This can be done by asking the teacher to name the practices they embedded in their instruction or by stating that you noticed one of the practices. Either way, this framing of the conversation enables both you and the teacher to put aside other thoughts and concerns about the lesson and focus exclusively on student engagement in the science practices—more specifically, on one particular practice.

Probing questions. Often, after establishing the focus of the conversion, there is a tendency to launch directly into feedback. However, taking the time to ask questions is crucial to maintaining a productive conference and more deeply understanding the teacher's rationale for his or her instructional decisions. Therefore, we recommend that you ask specific, probing questions intended to draw out the teacher's thinking around the focal science practice and how it was embedded in the instruction. The answers will provide you with a broader picture of instruction and a more nuanced understanding of the teacher's goals and decisions. Examples include "Tell me a little bit about why you decided to do X when students were engaged in [science practice]?" and "Why were students in groups for X part of the lesson but working individually for Y part of the lesson? How did this support their participation in [science practice]?"

Key levers. Now it is time to offer feedback. Make your feedback specific to what you observed during the lesson and rooted in the language of the continuum. See if you can identify a specific piece of feedback that will most dramatically improve the teacher's performance. Try to be as concise and concrete as possible as you share your feedback. The goal here is to support the teacher as he or she shifts instruction toward higher levels on the continuum without making the feedback feel like personal criticism.

Future plans. After providing specific feedback, it is crucial that the teacher understands how to act on it and put it into action in the classroom. One way to do this is by recommending specific strategies the teacher can try out right away. The Instructional Strategies Tool (introduced in the next section) provides specific ideas for each science practice. You can suggest specific strategies to try or ask the teacher to pick one or more appropriate strategies. Before concluding, decide when you and the teacher will meet again to discuss progress and when you will schedule another observation. Share what you will look for in that next observation so the teacher knows what to expect.

Use the Instructional Strategies Tool

This tool provides you and your teachers with small, easy-to-implement strategies designed to improve instruction of the science practices (see Appendix C). Each version of the tool (one for each science practice) starts with a definition and then presents different practical strategies for use in the classroom. Keep in mind that this is not an exhaustive list, and you or your teachers will likely come up with additional strategies that work with some or all students that are definitely worth trying. The suggested strategies form a good starting point for new (or new-to-teaching-science-practices) teachers—or for teachers looking for concrete ideas to try in their classrooms.

Practice Using the Tools

Now that we have explained the feedback tools, let's look at an example of how they are used during the supervision cycle. The following vignette comes from Ms. Bridgewater's 6th grade classroom. The class is learning about adaptation and natural selection. Ms. Bridgewater introduces a set of data to students about black and green bugs that live in grassy areas and are hunted by birds. Recently, pollution from a nearby power plant has altered the color of the grass in some areas of the habitat, changing it from green to black. The assistant principal, Ms. Manuel, stops in to observe the class.

Ms. Bridgewater: I'm passing out the data to you that we just talked about. You are getting a graph showing what the bug population has been for the last few years and a data table showing how much pollution has been coming from the power plant. There are also pictures of this environment. One picture is from 10 years ago, one is from 5 years ago, and one is from last year. Your job today is to use these data and work with your group to answer this question: Will the pollution affect the bugs?

Ms. Manuel walks around and listens to one group of students.

Leslie: The graph here shows that for the past few years, there have been way more black bugs than green bugs.

Juan: Wow. Look at these pictures! The grass was green 10 years ago, but now it has some spots that are turning black. Cool.

Leslie: I've never seen black grass before. I wonder why it turned black.

Sadie: Is it because of the pollution? So the answer is that the pollution will affect the bugs?

Juan: Sounds good to me.

Ms. Manuel moves and listens to another group.

Joshua: The question is will the pollution affect the bugs.

Daniel: Probably, right? I mean, pollution affects everything.

Isabel: I think we should look at the graph.

Joshua: The graph shows that there have always been way more green bugs than black bugs. What does that have to do with pollution?

Isabel: I wonder if the pollution will make there be more black bugs than green bugs.

Daniel: Maybe the pollution will make red bugs appear!

As Ms. Manuel leaves, Ms. Bridgewater calls the students back together to discuss their work.

After the observation, Ms. Manuel goes back to her office to consider what she saw and what the post-observation conference with Ms.

Bridgewater, scheduled for later that afternoon, should look like. Now is also a good time for you to consider what feedback you would provide to Ms. Bridgewater. Here are some questions to guide your thinking:

- Which science practice(s) did you notice?
- Where would you put these practices on the continuum?
- What specific recommendations would you make to Ms. Bridgewater to help her move her instruction further on the continuum for these practices?

We noticed that Ms. Bridgewater attempted to engage students in two science practices in this vignette: Analyzing and Interpreting Data and Constructing Explanations. We would put her instruction of the former practice at a Level 2 on the continuum because students had an opportunity to engage with three different representations of data, but they were not pushed to notice patterns in those data. For the latter science practice, we think the instruction fell at a Level 1. The students were asked to answer a question using data (Will the pollution affect the bugs?), but they did not actually create any explanations during the observed portion of the class. In addition, students seemed confused about the connection to pollution, so they were unable to use the data to support their answers.

Our recommendation in situations such as this—where there are multiple practices that need improvement—is to select one to focus on during the post-observation conference. It is important for the teacher to leave the conference with something small and concrete to work on.

Ms. Manuel completes the Post-Observation Conference Worksheet to help structure her conversation with Ms. Bridgewater (see Figure 5.1). Notice that in the Future Plans section, Ms. Manuel is prepared to offer two different suggestions for improvement, depending on what she learns in the conference. If she learns that Ms. Bridgewater did not engage students in Constructing Explanations because she needs to learn more about what counts as a scientific explanation, then she can direct her to a resource that can help her learn this. However, if she understands scientific explanations but not how to help students create them, then the Instructional Strategies Tool could be helpful.

FIGURE 5.1 : Ms. Manuel's Post-Observation Conference Worksheet

Post-Observation Conference Worksheet

Educator Name: Ms. Bridgewater   Observation Date:

Agenda Overview	Preparation for Conference	Notes from Conference
Praise *Deliver specific praise, and reference an area in which the teacher demonstrated growth in use of the science practices.*	Different displays of data. Students worked well in groups.	
Focal Science Practices *Identify the science practices observed and this conference's focal practice.*	Analyzing Data Constructing Explanations Focus on explanations.	
Probing Questions *Ask a probing question that gets to your "key lever" around the focal science practice.*	Were students able to write scientific explanations? How could you get students to write explanations that explain how/why the bug population will change?	
Key Levers *Deliver the piece of feedback that will most dramatically improve the teacher's performance around the focal science practice.*	The question Ms. Bridgewater posed did not seem to require an explanation—just a yes/no answer. A better question would help students write explanations.	
Future Plans *Identify the resources that will improve the focal science practice. Discuss follow-up observations and what you will look for.*	If Ms. Bridgewater does not understand what explanations are, suggest looking at NGSS webinars. If she understands scientific explanations but not how to help students create them, share the handout of instructional strategies for this practice.	

Ms. Bridgewater and Ms. Manuel meet later that afternoon to discuss the lesson Ms. Manuel observed.

Ms. Manuel: Tell me a little about how you think the lesson went.

Ms. Bridgewater: It was pretty good. I mean, the kids were using all that data.

Ms. Manuel: I was impressed that you were able to find data in three different formats for your students to use. I know that we have been working on moving beyond just data tables to display data.

Ms. Bridgewater: Yeah, I was especially interested to see how they would use those pictures of the environment. I hoped they would see that the grass was starting to turn black and relate that to the data showing an increase in pollution.

Ms. Manuel: So, clearly analyzing data was one science practice you were focusing on today. Anything else?

Ms. Bridgewater: Actually, I was also trying to get the students to write scientific explanations. I wanted them to use all that data to create a claim that answers the question.

Ms. Manuel: Then let's focus on that practice. Did you think the students were able to create scientific explanations?

Ms. Bridgewater: They answered the question I gave them. I mean, most groups said yes, the pollution affects the bugs, but they didn't really seem like explanations. I know that scientific explanations should be about how or why a phenomenon happens. I wanted the students to use the data and explain how they think the pollution might cause the populations of the green and black bugs to change.

Ms. Manuel: I agree. I listened to two different groups, and like you said, they answered the question but didn't go much beyond that. How do you think you could get students to address the "how" aspect?

Ms. Bridgewater: I wonder if an important first step is just making sure the students know what it means to write a scientific explanation. I just assumed they would support their claims, but I think I should be much clearer with them about what makes their answer a scientific explanation.

Ms. Manuel: I agree. Clear expectations are really important. Also, I wonder about the question you asked: "Will the pollution affect the bugs?" That sounds like it is asking for a yes or no answer instead of an explanation about how the pollution might affect the bugs.

Ms. Bridgewater: Hmmm. That makes sense. Do you think I should change it?

Ms. Manuel: Look here at Numbers 2 and 3 on this Instructional Strategies Tool.

Ms. Bridgewater: OK, those make sense. First, I could introduce the idea of a scientific explanation and maybe make a poster to hang in the room that says the goal of a scientific explanation is to explain how or why something occurs. Then I will make sure that the questions I ask really align with writing an explanation.

Ms. Manuel: I like that plan. I am planning to be back in your room in three weeks. Can you let me know when a good time is to stop in and see you teach about explanations again?

Ms. Bridgewater: Absolutely. I'll email you.

As we mentioned, it is often best to pick one practice on which to focus during the post-observation conference so the teacher leaves with a few concrete steps to try in the classroom. In this case, Ms. Manuel and Ms. Bridgewater focus on Constructing Explanations. During the conversation, Ms. Manuel learns that Ms. Bridgewater understands what constitutes a scientific explanation but needs support to implement it in the classroom. Therefore, they agree that over the next few weeks, Ms. Bridgewater will teach students what counts as a scientific explanation and work to provide students with questions rooted in explaining why a phenomenon occurs.

Figure 5.2 shows the completed Post-Observation Conference Worksheet, including Ms. Manuel's notes from the conference. These notes will be useful in focusing subsequent observations of Ms. Bridgewater's instruction.

FIGURE 5.2 : Ms. Manuel's Completed Post-Observation Conference Worksheet

Post-Observation Conference Worksheet

Educator Name: Ms. Bridgewater   Observation Date:

Agenda Overview	Preparation for Conference	Notes from Conference
Praise *Deliver specific praise, and reference an area in which the teacher demonstrated growth in use of the science practices.*	Different displays of data Students worked well in groups.	Ms. Bridgewater has been working on providing different displays of data.
Focal Science Practices *Identify the science practices observed and this conference's focal practice.*	Analyzing Data Constructing Explanations Focus on explanations	Ms. Bridgewater understands that explanations should focus on how or why a phenomenon occurs, but she is struggling with how to get students to do this.
Probing Questions *Ask a probing question that gets to your "key lever" around the focal science practice.*	Were students able to write scientific explanations? How could you get students to write explanations that explain how/why the bug population will change?	
Key Levers *Deliver the piece of feedback that will most dramatically improve the teacher's performance around the focal science practice.*	The question Ms. Bridgewater posed did not seem to require an explanation—just a yes/no answer. A better question would help students write explanations.	Ms. Bridgewater will work on writing questions. She will also teach students what constitutes a scientific explanation so the expectations are clear.
Future Plans *Identify the resources that will improve the focal science practice. Discuss follow-up observations and what you will look for.*	If Ms. Bridgewater does not understand what explanations are, suggest looking at NGSS webinars. If she understands scientific explanations but not how to help students create them, share the handout of instructional strategies for this practice.	Since Ms. Bridgewater has a good understanding of what a scientific explanation is, she will use the next few weeks to teach it more explicitly to students and write better questions. Observe again in approximately 3 weeks.

Two weeks later, Ms. Bridgewater emails Ms. Manuel to let her know that the following week she will be teaching a lesson that focuses on scientific explanations. This time, students will be using data about birds with different types of beaks to create explanations about which bird species will have the most offspring.

Ms. Manuel enters the classroom just as Ms. Bridgewater projects the following on the board: "Write a <u>scientific explanation</u>: Which species of birds will have the most offspring?"

Ms. Bridgewater: Before we start answering this question, let's remind ourselves what makes our answers to this question a scientific explanation. Kendra?

Kendra: A scientific explanation should tell why something happens. In this case, why does the type of bird have the most babies?

Ms. Bridgewater: Exactly. Your job is to use the two data tables that show how much the different types of birds eat and the kinds of flowers and seeds present in the environment. Of course, you should also use what you know about adaptation and survival to explain why the bird type you chose will have the most offspring. Where can you look if you forget what makes something a scientific explanation?

Gustavo: That poster on the wall. [See Figure 5.3.]

Ms. Bridgewater: Good. Today, you are each going to write your own explanation. Tomorrow, you will have a chance to share your explanations and give with one another feedback.

Kendra: Can we change them after that?

Ms. Bridgewater: Of course. That is what scientists do. They critique one another's work so everyone's work gets better. But today, focus on making sure your explanation uses data to explain why you think one species of bird will have the most offspring.

> *The students write. Ms. Manuel asks to read Jill's and Luke's explanation when they are done to offer them personal feedback. [See Figure 5.4.]*

FIGURE 5.3 : Scientific Explanations Poster

SCIENTIFIC EXPLANATIONS show *how* or *why* something happens.

1. Make a claim. (Answer the question.)

2. Support your claim with
   • Evidence (such as measurements, observations)
   • Reasoning (Why does this evidence support the claim?)

FIGURE 5.4 : Sample Student Explanations

Jill's Explanation:

My claim is that the bird with the longest beak will have the most offspring. The first data table shows that there are lots of flowers with nectar inside for food. The second data table shows that birds with long beaks can eat this food. If they have a lot of food and the other birds with shorter beaks can't get this food, then the long-beak birds will survive. The birds that survive will have the most babies. The babies will also have long beaks. Having a long beak is an adaptation that makes the bird survive.

Luke's Explanation:

I think the bird with the long beak will have more babies. The bird with the most food will probably have the most babies because you need food to live. There are flowers that only the birds with long beaks can get the food out of. The other birds can't eat this food and so they have to find other food. There isn't as much of the other food so some of them might die. This is why I think the birds with the long beaks will have more babies.

Ms. Manuel once again returns to her office to reflect on what she observed and plan the post-observation conference. What feedback would you provide to Ms. Bridgewater this time? Here are some questions to guide your thinking:

• Did students engage in Constructing Explanations?
• Where would you put Ms. Bridgewater's instruction of this science practice on the continuum?
• What next steps would you recommend to Ms. Bridgewater?

It's clear that Ms. Bridgewater's instruction of Constructing Explanations has certainly improved. In the initial observation, we did not see students creating explanations. The question she asked required a yes or no answer, and students did not know how to connect the data to their answers. During the follow-up observation, however, we can see that Ms. Bridgewater has taught students what constitutes a scientific explanation and provided a poster on the wall to remind them of its components. She also explicitly states that students should use the data from the data tables as evidence—along with science ideas from the readings as reasoning—to justify their claims. It is also important to note that the question Ms. Bridgewater asks the class cannot be answered with a simple yes or no. It requires students to select the species that will have the most offspring and explain why they selected that species.

In looking at the two students' explanations, we see that Jill can use evidence from the data tables and reasoning about what counts as an adaptation in her explanation. Luke's explanation is logical, and his claim is accurate, but he does not use data from the data tables as evidence. For these reasons, we would rate this lesson at a Level 3 on the continuum.

Ms. Manuel should certainly offer a great deal of praise to Ms. Bridgewater about the growth in her instruction relevant to this science practice. The second post-observation conference should focus on how to help Luke (and other students like him) include evidence and reasoning in his explanation. Ms. Manuel might direct Ms. Bridgewater to the Instructional Strategies Tool for Constructing Explanations and recommend Strategy 5 (provide scaffolds such as sentence frames) or Strategy 6 (have students highlight features of an explanation in their writing) to help Luke notice areas for improvement.

A Few Practical Tips

Use the Feedback Tools Flexibly

The tools we presented in this chapter are designed to help you structure these important conversations with teachers, but you know your teachers and school culture best. The Post-Observation Conference Worksheet is in a specific order to encourage discussion about the observation so the eventual feedback is meaningful to the teacher and most likely to improve student learning. However, you should feel free to make changes as necessary. For example, if you notice more than one strength worth mentioning, praise the teacher on multiple fronts! If you prefer to start the conference by asking the teacher to reflect on the lesson, that is fine as well. If you see something unrelated to the science practices that needs attention, it is OK to begin or finish the conference with a brief discussion about it.

Use the tools flexibly so they meet your unique needs and the needs of your teachers and school. Our only caution is that any changes you make should maintain a focus on the science practices and on moving teachers' instruction forward along the continuum. We've seen well-intentioned teachers and principals modify the continuum so it cuts across more disciplines, but the result is the science practices are no longer the focus. Similarly, we've heard from principals and other observers who fail to see value in the continuum because there are so many other good things happening in the classroom. In each of these cases, taking the time to revisit student goals usually helps everyone refocus on the science practices.

Use the Language of the Continuum

To enable a discussion rooted in the science practices, it is important to have copies of the continuum to reference during the post-observation conference. We have found that pointing to and using the language of the continuum with teachers helps ensure the conversation does not get off track. Likewise, we have noticed that the more principals and other observers use the continuum explicitly with teachers, the more teachers internalize what it means to improve their instruction. One teacher shared with us that she keeps the language of the continuum in mind when she is teaching and can often realize when she is veering toward a lower rather than a higher level.

Prioritize Follow-Ups

The most important part of the entire observation and feedback process is what happens in the classroom after the post-observation conference. It's critical that you get back into the teacher's classroom to observe again and have another post-observation conference. Some schools have implemented regular schedules of observations and post-observation conferences—sometimes with the principal, sometimes with another supervisor or coach. In other schools, teachers are provided with a year-long schedule of when they will meet with a supervisor or coach so they can anticipate the supervision cycles. Another model we've seen is one in which principals and coaches rotate through groups of teachers so teachers get feedback from more than one individual. Whatever structure you use in your school, short, frequent observations have been found to be far more effective than infrequent, longer ones (Bambrick-Santoyo, 2012).

Returning to Mr. Stuart

Dr. Dean returns to her office and takes out a copy of the Post-Observation Conference Worksheet. She decides to start the conference with Mr. Stuart with praise about student engagement and Mr. Stuart's encouragement of students' questions. Since the focal science practice was clearly Asking Questions, Dr. Dean plans to focus on how Mr. Stuart might support students in asking scientific questions. She looks at the Instructional Strategies Tool for Asking Questions and sees two strategies that could help Mr. Stuart's students understand what counts as a scientific question and then ask those types of questions. She plans to show these to Mr. Stuart if he does not bring up similar ideas. Dr. Dean also notes that if Mr. Stuart does not understand what counts as a scientific question, she will suggest that he talk to Mrs. Robertson, a 2nd grade teacher who recently worked to improve her instruction of this practice. Dr. Dean feels prepared for the upcoming conference and is looking forward to the discussion with Mr. Stuart.

Discussion Questions

Reflection

1. What are two takeaways from this chapter?
2. Think of a post-observation conference you have conducted in the past. How did you prepare for it? What was the focus?
3. What type of feedback do you typically offer teachers? How is it similar to and different from the type of feedback encouraged by this chapter?
4. How do you think the Instructional Strategies Tool could be useful to you and teachers beyond post-observation conferences?

Application

1. How might you start using the tools described in this chapter in your observations and feedback?
2. What type of practice or rehearsal might you do before using these tools with teachers? With whom could you do this?
3. Changing the way you conduct post-observation conferences is challenging. What small changes might you try first? Why do these seem to be the easiest or most important to try?

6

Professional Development

Dr. Yim is excited to implement the new science-specific observation and feedback processes at George Washington Carver Elementary, where she is a principal. Since learning to look for the science practices in her teachers' classrooms and provide targeted, science-specific feedback, Dr. Yim has tried to regularly go into science classrooms at all grade levels. Unfortunately, she has found that her teachers are struggling to implement science lessons that really engage students in the practices. During preconferences, teachers talk about the ways they plan to engage their students in practices such as modeling and asking questions, but when Dr. Yim observes the classes, she finds that the teachers—rather than students—ask the questions, and they have students create overly descriptive models.

After reflecting on this pattern for a couple of weeks, Dr. Yim decides that she wants to use a portion of an upcoming in-service day to provide professional development for her teachers. She thinks her teachers could really benefit from targeted learning about the science practices, but she is overwhelmed with how to plan such a session. Dr. Yim used to be a 5th grade teacher and did not study science, so she does not feel overly confident running science-specific professional development.

However, her teachers responded poorly to outside facilitators in the past because the consultants did not have any idea what it was like to teach at their school specifically. Because of these issues, Dr. Yim decides to recruit her instructional leadership team to help run this professional development, but when they all meet, they realize they need some more resources to think about how to introduce these complex practices to the teachers.

Theorizing Professional Development: Considering Teachers' Experiences and Contexts

The supervision cycle is an important component of instructional leadership, but focusing exclusively on observation and feedback is often not enough to support substantial instructional reform. As Dr. Yim noted, many teachers can benefit from targeted professional development (PD) that supports their understanding of high-leverage reforms, such as the science practices.

We also know that many teachers have struggled with lecture-based PD or PD that is disconnected from teachers' experiences and context (Kennedy, 2016). In this chapter, therefore, we share our approach for designing PD sessions about the science practices that are engaging, collaborative, and teacher-centered. We believe one of the keys to good PD is considering how teachers might come to understand the science practices through the lens of their past experiences. We talk about this idea and then show how it might be used to create PD sessions that introduce the practices in general or focus on one particular practice in depth.

Professional development has long been used as a tool to help teachers improve their skills and knowledge, and many researchers have investigated how to make PD as effective as possible. From this work has come a generally accepted framework for five critical features of PD: content focus, active learning, coherence, duration, and collective participation (Desimone, 2009):

- **Content focus** means that PD should include learning activities centered around subject matter and how students learn those subjects.
- **Active learning** means that PD should include activities in which teachers are actively engaged in activities such as lesson planning, reflection, or analysis rather than simply listening to a presenter.
- **Coherence** means that what is learned during PD sessions should align with teachers' existing knowledge, beliefs, and experiences.
- **Duration** means that PD should be sufficiently long in terms of both the number of hours and the span of time over which it is presented. (Frustratingly, research has yet to agree on how long that is.)
- **Collective participation** means that PD is most effective when groups of teachers from the same context (e.g., school, grade, department) attend and learn together.

We clearly agree that content-specific PD can have a positive impact on teachers' practice and students' understanding, and features such as active learning and collective participation are basic hallmarks of good teaching. We think it is important to focus on the idea of coherence since it can be a key difference between PD that teachers find useful and engaging and PD they find frustrating and unnecessary. Research suggests that teachers make sense of PD based on their own teaching and accountability contexts, which means the way they understand new instructional strategies, tools, or policies will be informed by things they are already doing (Coburn, 2001).

Given the scale of instructional shifts mandated by the NGSS, it is particularly important for instructional leaders to attend to the experiences and ideas their teachers bring to science PD. Teachers typically respond to NGSS PD sessions by focusing on areas of coherence and incoherence between the NGSS and their unique instructional and organizational contexts (Allen & Penuel, 2015). Unfortunately, when teachers see large areas of incoherence, especially between the ways in which the PD asks them to teach and the values embedded in their school's observation and accountability systems, they are less likely to adopt the approach espoused by the PD (Allen & Penuel, 2015).

Thankfully, researchers have also found the opposite to be true. When teachers engage in PD in which the instructional reforms, accountability messages, and classroom experiences are aligned, they tend to learn more from the experience and their students demonstrate better performance on assessments of science abilities (Geier et al., 2008; Harris et al., 2015).

Therefore, instructional leaders have the necessary tools to support strong teacher learning if they acknowledge the experiences teachers bring to PD sessions and set up opportunities to recognize coherence between new approaches to instruction and the methods of supervision leaders will use to hold them accountable. This is where we hope our tools are particularly helpful; as you use our tools to improve your supervision of the science practices, you can align them with the messages you convey through PD about those same practices.

Planning Professional Development

We know it can be overwhelming to plan PD around a topic as broad as the science practices, so we suggest beginning by limiting your focus. Focus on one science practice (or one group of science practices) at a time. There is a lot to unpack for each practice; therefore, we have found PD sessions that aim to address all eight tend to suffer from the classic "mile wide, inch deep" problem.

As discussed, it is important for your PD to meet your teachers where they are and consider their past experiences and current contexts. We cannot possibly know your teachers' context as well as you do, but we have found that teachers tend to fall into one of two general categories. Sometimes, teachers struggle to understand what a particular practice really means (or, in the case of elementary school teachers, what it means *for science*). If your teachers have this problem, then we suggest planning an "introduction to a science practice" PD session. We walk through an example of such a session in the next section and provide templates for sessions that might serve as an introduction to any of the eight practices.

Other groups of teachers have a good grasp of what a particular science practice means but need more support in thinking about how to make changes to their existing classroom structures and activities in order to support students in that practice. These teachers tend to benefit from PD that focuses on lesson adaptations (Cherbow, McNeill, Lowenhaupt, McKinley, & Lowell, 2019). In these sessions, teachers examine various ways other teachers have implemented a science practice in the classroom and use the continuum to rank and discuss those adaptations. Later in this chapter, we share an example of this kind of PD and point you to templates for more.

Introduction to a Science Practice

If you find that your teachers are confused by or misunderstand a science practice, this type of PD session is a good place to start. Some of the science practices, such as Asking Questions or Developing and Using Models, use language that may be familiar to teachers from other disciplines but have a distinct meaning in science instruction. Another indication that this might be an appropriate type of PD session to run is if you find teachers using definitions from other disciplines when thinking about a particular science practice.

Our introduction to a science practices PD agenda is built on the idea that teachers will develop their understanding of the science practices by examining and reflecting on classroom instruction that features those practices. To that end, we have three main goals for these PD sessions:

1. Introduce teachers to the science practice and the different levels on the continuum.
2. Reflect on the use of the practice in classrooms.
3. Identify specific strategies that teachers might use to support that practice moving forward.

We believe that teachers need at least 90 minutes to dive into this work effectively, so we've designed a generic agenda for this introductory PD, which you can find in Figure 6.1.

We find this PD to be a helpful way to get teachers thinking about the science practices in general—and about how one practice appears in classroom instruction. If you find yourself with more than 90 minutes, you can add activities in which teachers experience a lesson that engages in the practice well, critique or revise a lesson plan you provide, or work together to design a lesson that asks students to engage in the focal practice.

FIGURE 6.1 : Generic Introduction to a Science Practice PD Agenda

Activity	Description	Time
Overview and Introductions	• Provide an overview of the workshop. • Have everyone introduce themselves (including their familiarity with the NGSS science practices).	10 min
Presentation of Materials and Definitions	• Introduce the vision of science as a set of practices. • Introduce the focal science practice(s) for the day (e.g., Developing and Using Models). • Share NGSS science practices definitions from ILSP (www.sciencepracticesleadership.com/definitions.html). • Share the Science Practices Continuum and discuss its use (www.sciencepracticesleadership.com/continuum.html). *Handouts: definitions of all eight practices, Science Practices Continuum*	20 min
Activity #1: Case Study	• Shared a video/vignette that is high on the continuum for the focal practice(s). • Select and watch the video, or read the vignette individually or in pairs for the target science practice. • Using the definitions, identify all practices that students engaged in during instruction. • Using the continuum, identify the level of the focal practice shown in instruction.	10 min
Reflection	• Engage in whole-group or partner/small-group discussion. – What practices did you see in the lesson the way it was taught? What was your evidence? – Where did you put the focal practice on the continuum? Why? – In what ways did the teacher support the focal practice? How could the teacher have better supported it? • Distribute the Instructional Strategies Tool for the focal practice and give teachers an opportunity to discuss which strategies might have value for the lesson and how they might be scaffolded for students. *Handouts: Instructional Strategy Tool for focal practice(s)*	15 min
Activity #2: Case Study	• Shared a video/vignette that is low on the continuum for the focal practice(s). • Select and watch the video, or read the vignette individually or in pairs for the target science practice. • Using the definitions, identify all practices that students engaged in during instruction. • Using the continuum, identify the level of the focal practice shown in instruction.	10 min

(continued)

FIGURE 6.1 : Generic Introduction to a Science Practice PD Agenda—*(continued)*

Activity	Description	Time
Reflection and Comparison	• Engage in whole-group or partner/small-group discussion. – What practices did you see in the lesson the way it was taught? What was your evidence? – Where did you put the focal practice on the continuum? Why? – How were these videos/vignettes similar? – How were they different? – Which do you think is similar to the ways you currently teach? Why? – What supports would help you incorporate the focal practice into your instruction?	15 min
Conclusions	• Discuss. – Questions – Major takeaways – Plans for classroom instruction – Plans for follow-up and sharing with colleagues	10 min

After observing and having post-observation conversations with multiple teachers, Dr. Yim realizes that many of her teachers seem to be applying a generic content-neutral understanding to the term *modeling*. They think of modeling as teachers demonstrating how to do something to students or as students using a drawing to describe a scientific idea they have memorized.

Dr. Yim knows, however, that scientific modeling involves students using their own thinking to explain how or why something happens in the natural world. Because of this issue, she decides to plan an introductory PD session on the science practice of Developing and Using Models.

After securing 90 minutes during the next in-service day, Dr. Yim and her instructional leadership team create an agenda for an "Introduction to Scientific Modeling" session (Figure 6.2).

FIGURE 6.2 : Dr. Yim's Introduction to Scientific Modeling Agenda

Activity	Description	Time
Overview and Introductions	• Provide an overview of the workshop. • Have everyone introduce themselves (including their familiarity with modeling in science).	10 min
Presentation of Materials and Definitions	• Introduce the vision of science as a set of practices. • Introduce the focus on Developing and Using Models. • Share NGSS science practices definitions from ILSP (www.sciencepracticesleadership.com/definitions.html). • Share the Science Practices Continuum and discuss its use (www.sciencepracticesleadership.com/continuum.html). *Handouts: definitions of all eight practices, Science Practices Continuum*	20 min

Activity #1: Case Study	• Share a video that shows strong modeling.
	• Show a video of 3rd grade students engaged in modeling in a unit on sound (www.sciencepractices leadership.com/video---grade-3-ii.html).
	• After the video, teachers work in small groups to
	  – Identify all practices that students engaged in during the video.
	  – Identify the level on the continuum they observed for the practice of Developing and Using Models.
	  – Explain why they assigned the level they did.
		10 min

Reflection	• Engage in small-group discussion.
	  – What practices did you see in the lesson the way it was taught? What was your evidence?
	  – Where did you put Developing and Using Models on the continuum? Why?
	  – In what ways did the teacher support modeling? How could the teacher have better supported it?
	• Distribute the Instructional Strategies Tool for Developing and Using Models and give teachers an opportunity to discuss in small groups which strategies might have value for the lesson and how they might be scaffolded for students.
	• Share out to the whole group the results of the small-group discussions.
	
	Handout: Instructional Strategy Tool for Developing and Using Models
		15 min

(continued)

FIGURE 6.2 : Dr. Yim's Introduction to Scientific Modeling Agenda—*(continued)*

Activity	Description	Time
Activity #2: Case Study	• Share a video that shows weak modeling. • Pass out the lesson adaptation for teachers to read (www.sciencepracticesleadership.com/lesson-adaptation---grade-2.html). • After reading the vignette, teachers work in small groups to – Identify all practices that students engaged in during the vignette. – Identify the level on the continuum they observed for the practice of Developing and Using Models. – Explain why they assigned the level they did.	10 min
Reflection and Comparison	• Engage in small-group discussion. – What practices did you see in the lesson the way it was taught? What was your evidence? – Where did you put Developing and Using Models on the continuum? Why? – In what ways did the teacher support modeling? How could the teacher have better supported it? – How were these case studies similar? – How were they different? – Which do you think is similar to the ways you currently teach? Why? – What supports would help you incorporate a focus on modeling into your instruction? • Share out to the whole group the results of the small-group discussions.	15 min
Conclusions	• Ask teachers to share one major takeaway and one question they had from the PD session. • Provide an exit ticket to each teacher with the following questions: – How did this session help you develop your understanding of scientific modeling? – What plans do you have to incorporate scientific modeling in your classroom? – What further support do you need?	10 min

Lesson Adaptations

Sometimes teachers have a good understanding of a particular science practice but are unsure how to implement the practice in their classrooms. The practices are complex and multifaceted, so it is reasonable that teachers might find it difficult to fully unpack them. Alternatively, teachers might feel unable to find or come up with examples of what a particular practice should look like in the classroom.

These teachers will likely not find the introductory PD session very helpful. In its place, we recommend a session that allows them to work with specific examples of a practice in use and then think about how they might apply that practice to their own classroom. Our lesson adaptation PD addresses these needs by asking teachers to read four versions of the same lesson; each represents a different level on the Science Practices Continuum (see Figure 6.3). By looking at variations of the same practice, teachers can begin to see how a lesson could be adapted to better support students as they engage in that practice. Given that this PD session assumes teachers already have some familiarity with the relevant science practice, we believe it can be effective in 60 minutes.

FIGURE 6.3 : Generic Lesson Adaptation PD Agenda

Activity	Description	Time
Overview and Introductions	• Provide an overview of the workshop and its objectives, including the focal science practice. • Have everyone introduce themselves (including their familiarity with the focal practice).	5 min
Review Continuum	• Pass out the Science Practices Continuum and discuss its use (www.sciencepracticesleadership.com/continuum.html). • In pairs/small groups, give teachers time to read the continuum for the focal practice and discuss the key things that distinguish each level from the next. • Ask small groups to share out to the whole group what they discussed and any initial questions that came up from reviewing the continuum. *Handout: Science Practices Continuum*	10 min
Introduce Lesson Adaptation	• Pass out a lesson adaptation packet for the focal practice (www.sciencepracticesleadership.com/lesson-adaptation.html). • Introduce the context for the lesson, found on the first page of the lesson adaptation. *Handout: Lesson Adaptation Packet for focal practice*	5 min
Read Lesson Adaptation	• Teachers individually read the lesson adaptation and record responses to the following questions: – Where would you rank this on the continuum? – What specific evidence from the adaptation supports your ranking?	5 min

(continued)

FIGURE 6.3 : Generic Lesson Adaptation PD Agenda—(*continued*)

Activity	Description	Time
Discussion of Rankings	• In small groups, teachers discuss the following questions: – How did you rank each lesson? – What specific evidence led to your rankings? – What questions or concerns came up while ranking? • Ask volunteers to share out takeaways from their small-group discussions. Explore any disagreements or confusions that came up while reading the adaptations.	15 min
Takeaways and Application	• Engage in partner/small-group discussions. – How has this improved your understanding of the focal practice? – What questions do you still have about supporting students to engage in the focal practice? – What is one specific way you can adapt your classroom instruction to better support students to engage in the focal practice? • Ask each small group to share out their specific adaptation idea. Collect these on a poster or an electronic document that you can share with teachers after the session.	15 min
Conclusions	• Summarize group takeaways. • Look ahead to future work. • Provide an exit ticket to each participant with the following questions: – What is one thing you learned from this PD? – What suggestions do you have for improving future PD? – What further support do you need?	5 min

We find this PD is a helpful way to develop teachers' understanding of a science practice and help them consider how it might look (or not look) in a classroom. Note that the goal is not for teachers to all agree on how the adaptations are ranked (or even for them to get the same answer as we expected when we wrote them) but rather to provide a space for teachers to see and discuss what it might look like to move toward a classroom in which students are more actively using the science practices to figure out something about the natural world.

If you find that you have more time, you might consider adding in an analysis of a video case study or giving teachers more time to modify one of their own lessons to better support the focal practice. The more you can support teachers in connecting their understanding of the science practice with their own work in the classroom—and your methods of supervising their instruction—the more helpful they will find the PD session.

A few months after completing the introductory PD session, Dr. Yim finds that her teachers feel much more confident with what many of the practices mean for science. However, as she talks to them, she finds that many of them still find Analyzing and Interpreting Data difficult because they are unsure how to balance scaffolding interpretation with giving students an opportunity to do their own analyses.

Based on this feedback, Dr. Yim and her instructional leadership team decide to use the lesson adaptation PD session to focus on Analyzing and Interpreting Data. They create the agenda seen in Figure 6.4.

FIGURE 6.4 : Dr. Yim's Lesson Adaptation PD Agenda

Activity	Description	Time
Overview and Introductions	• Provide an overview of the workshop and its objectives, including Analyzing and Interpreting Data. • Have everyone introduce themselves (including their familiarity with Analyzing and Interpreting Data).	5 min
Review Continuum	• Pass out the Science Practices Continuum and discuss its use (www.sciencepracticesleadership.com/continuum.html). • In pairs/small groups, give teachers time to read the continuum for Analyzing and Interpreting Data and discuss the key things that distinguish each level from the next. • Ask small groups to share out to the whole group what they discussed and any initial questions that came up from reviewing the continuum. *Handout: Science Practices Continuum*	10 min

(continued)

FIGURE 6.4 : Dr. Yim's Lesson Adaptation PD Agenda—(*continued*)

Activity	Description	Time
Introduce Lesson Adaptation	• Pass out a lesson adaptation packet for Analyzing and Interpreting Data (www.sciencepractices leadership.com/lesson-adaptation---grade-3.html). • Introduce the context for the lesson: a 3rd grade class looking at temperature/precipitation data during various seasons. *Handout: Lesson Adaptation Packet for Analyzing and Interpreting Data*	5 min
Read Lesson Adaptation	• Teachers individually read the lesson adaptation and record responses to the following questions: – Where would you rank this on the continuum? – What specific evidence from the adaptation supports your ranking?	5 min
Discussion of Rankings	• In small groups, teachers discuss the following questions: – How did you rank each lesson? – What specific evidence led to your rankings? – What questions or concerns came up while ranking? • Ask volunteers to share out takeaways from their small-group discussions. Explore any disagreements or confusions that came up while reading the adaptations.	15 min
Takeaways and Application	• Engage in partner/small-group discussions. – How has this improved your understanding of Analyzing and Interpreting Data? – What questions do you still have about supporting students to engage in Analyzing and Interpreting Data? – What is one specific way you can adapt your classroom instruction to better support students to engage in Analyzing and Interpreting Data? • Ask each small group to share out their specific adaptation idea. Collect these on a poster or an electronic document that you can share with teachers after the session.	15 min
Conclusions	• Summarize group takeaways. • Connect to PLC work happening at the school. • Provide an exit ticket to each participant with the following questions: – What is one thing you learned from this PD? – What suggestions do you have for improving future PD? – What further support do you need?	5 min

A Few Practical Tips

Use the Expertise in Your Building

Teachers often respond well to PD run by people they already know and trust, and the closer the session is to their lived reality, the more likely they are to adopt ideas from the PD. For these reasons, we encourage you to look to the people already in your building or district to see if they can facilitate the PD sessions. Because our recommended PD sessions focus on teachers working together to think through practical examples of the science practices, your facilitators need not be total experts in the practices. The more they can embody the idea that instructional improvement is a joint learning process, the more you can create opportunities for effective teacher learning.

In our experience, when teachers from different schools and grade levels work together and participate in regular meetings and professional development sessions, they return to their schools and teams reinvigorated and eager to share and model what they learned. This accomplishes three goals. First, it promotes consistency across schools because all these teacher leaders are participating in common experiences. Second, it gives the PD leader a sense of what is happening across multiple schools and grades, which is helpful for planning districtwide PD. Finally, regular meetings/PD sessions provide information to frame conversations with principals.

Focus on One Practice or Group of Practices at a Time

The science practices are big and complex, and eight separate practices is a lot to wrap your head around at once. For that reason, we strongly recommend you avoid the temptation to address all eight simultaneously; that will likely overwhelm your teachers and reduce the chances they will make positive instructional changes. Take small bites. Focus on one practice or group of practices you think is critical for your building or will help teachers think across science, literacy, and math. This focused approach will allow teachers time to learn about and try new approaches to specific practices in a way that will feel more doable. Sometimes, the best first step might be an entire practice; other times, it might be a feature that cuts across several practices, such as student discourse or the use of evidence.

Align Your PD with Your Supervision

Even though this has been an overarching theme of this chapter, it is important to reiterate. Your teachers will know if the way you talk about instruction during a PD session does not align with the way you supervise them in their classrooms. For example, you can do plenty of PD asking teachers to give their students more control over the way they analyze data, but if your supervision focuses on each student getting the right answer as quickly as possible, then teachers will focus on what you are asking of them. Therefore, before you dive into PD, make sure you reflect on your own supervision practices to ensure the messages you are sending are aligned across supervision and PD.

Returning to Dr. Yim

After both the introductory and lesson adaptation PD sessions, Dr. Yim feels much better about her teachers' understanding and use of the science practices. She also realizes that she has become more confident in her own ability to facilitate science-specific PD, even though she never received formal training in science. During both sessions, her teachers had plenty of questions she could not answer, but they still appreciated seeing more strong classroom examples of the practices in action. This experience allowed Dr. Yim to be more open with her teachers, and she realizes she does not need to be an "expert" who tells them what to do. Rather, she needs to be someone who provides them with tools and resources to push their own understanding.

During the next few weeks, Dr. Yim realizes that she is seeing much more complex use of the science practices in classrooms and is having richer conversations about the practices during her post-observation conferences. Both she and her teachers still feel unsure about how exactly to reach the highest level of the continuum for each practice all the time, but they now have concrete next steps to continue building their thinking.

Discussion Questions

Reflection

1. What are two takeaways from this chapter?
2. Think of a positive PD experience you had in the past. What made it so successful?
3. How do you typically encourage teachers to develop their own skills and knowledge? What are some benefits and drawbacks of your current system of PD?
4. How can focusing on the science practices in PD be a lever for supporting instructional reform?

Application

1. How might you use the tools and PD agendas in this chapter to support teacher learning in your school?
2. What specific practice(s) do your teachers need support thinking about? Why do they need that support?
3. Would teachers in your building benefit from an introduction to science practices or looking at lesson adaptations? Why?
4. How could you use some of the other tools found in this book in other kinds of PD sessions?

7

Taking the First Steps

The supervision cycle and the Science Practices Continuum provide concrete, usable tools for leaders to work in partnership with teachers to understand and integrate the science practices into classrooms and schools. In the context of substantial instructional reform, ensuring that all educators have the resources they need to adapt their instruction is central to successful change. To enact the kind of deep reform the NGSS envisions requires a subject-specific approach to supervision. In recent years, as science has become marginalized as an untested subject in many schools, many K–8 teachers have not been provided with the support they need to create engaging science lessons and classrooms.

This is more urgent than ever. We have failed to offer meaningful and challenging science instruction to historically underserved communities, such as our students of color, students who are learning English, and students from low-income communities (Bang et al., 2017). Engaging students in the science practices as they make sense of natural phenomena offers new and more equitable opportunities for all students. The act of doing and speaking science as students conduct investigations, construct arguments from evidence, and evaluate different models can shift students' vision of what counts as science. Ultimately, students can see themselves and their peers as scientists who ask questions, share ideas, gather evidence, and figure out phenomena together as a classroom community.

Furthermore, engaging students in this work can offer teachers new opportunities to see, hear, and notice their students' sensemaking processes, including the rich resources they bring to the lesson from their personal experiences and communities outside school. This type of work can help teachers build relationships with their students and hear the brilliance in their students' scientific sensemaking, even when they are from different cultural, linguistic, or socioeconomic backgrounds (Brown, 2019). The science practices support culturally expansive learning that increases student engagement and sensemaking in science.

However, the promise of the science practices can only be met if instructional reform is implemented across the system, with supervisors learning alongside teachers and supporting them as they try out new pedagogical strategies and reframe instruction to integrate the practices. Of course, we cannot expect this to happen overnight! Both teachers and their supervisors need time to learn about and practice this new approach. It may feel daunting, but it is important to start somewhere. It's time to take the first step!

Rising to the Challenge

Implementing the science practices is no easy task. We expect a lot from teachers as we push them to change their science instruction substantially to engage students in these eight practices. Although some practices may be more familiar than others, their full implementation requires a rethinking of the pedagogy, content, and culture of science classrooms. Through our ongoing collaboration with instructional leaders, we have identified several key challenges that make the integration of the practices difficult. Although everyone's context is different, recognizing these challenges may help leaders identify strategies to overcome them in their work with teachers.

Potential Difficulties for Teachers

Instructional leaders need to recognize and address some of the most common reasons teachers have trouble adapting their practice to integrate the science practices:

- **Fewer topics are covered.** Implementing the science practices slows down the coverage of content. Teachers worry that engaging fully with the practices requires more time and means less content is covered. Therefore, leaders need to convey the value of engaging more fully in fewer topics, allowing students to participate in the science practices on a regular basis. Leaders should also encourage teachers to examine the NGSS (or state adaptation of the NGSS) and start to notice that there are in fact fewer topics—and students are expected to have deeper understandings of them. Embedding the practices into science instruction is a key for this to happen.

- **Eight is a lot!** As teachers implement a new framework, they find that eight is simply too many practices to keep track of or try at once. Teachers (and leaders) might initially think they have to do all eight practices in every lesson, which is not true and can lead to progress paralysis. Identify a few practices to focus on initially. We present groupings of practices that may be useful in this regard—and keep teachers from feeling overwhelmed. Keep in mind, though, that implementing the practices is a process that does not happen overnight or all at once.

- **But I already do this!** Some teachers feel as if they already engage in the science practices because of the array of hands-on activities they have in place. Teachers need time to reflect on how their existing hands-on activities do or do not integrate the science practices, since such activities often do not engage students in the science practices. In addition, some of the terms used by the practices mean different things in non-science contexts, which can cause confusion. For example, what it means to "model" in education in general is not the same as what it means to "model" in science, so teachers and supervisors may have a hard time understanding the content-specific nature of some of the practices. Leaders should address the meaning of various terms directly as they introduce and discuss the science practices with teachers.

- **How and when do I introduce the practices?** Teachers typically need help determining which routines to introduce and how to sequence those routines to gradually build students' ability to engage in the science practices. Some teachers worry that students need prior background knowledge to participate in the practices or are too young to engage in the practices. Others worry they are spending too much time on science when they should be teaching literacy. With all that in mind, leaders can point out that students develop background knowledge by engaging in the practices, and they can help teachers develop age-appropriate routines that allow early engagement with the practices. Through collaborative conversation, leaders and teachers can conceptualize the bridges between the science practices and practices in other subjects, including how the science practices amplify learning in other subjects.

Potential Difficulties for Leaders

Instructional leaders also face challenges when they try to support teachers:

- **Where do I find the time?** Instructional leaders wear many hats, and in K–8 contexts, they are most often school principals responsible for daily operations, supervising all subjects, and maintaining relationships with families and community members. One key challenge for them is carving out time to focus on supervising science—something that is often put on the back burner as they deal with the daily demands of leading schools. We suggest leaders plan and schedule time specifically for learning alongside teachers and supervising them in the science practices. This can take many forms, from attending collaborative teacher meetings already in place, to planning in-house professional development, to attending workshops about the science practices together. Our companion website (www.sciencepracticesleadership.com) offers suggestions and resources for in-house professional development. Narrow your focus and establish a goal of implementing only a few practices (or even just one) at a time. Furthermore, specifically scheduling time for the different steps of the supervision cycle is an important step to take.
- **I lack the appropriate expertise.** Leaders are often not science teachers. They are put in the position of supervising others

in the science practices before they themselves feel confident and fully understand the science practices. We recommend leaders be transparent with teachers about their background, learning, and development when it comes to implementing this reform. At first, their observations may focus on descriptions that can be discussed collaboratively with teachers.

- **How do I build motivation and trust?** Too often, leaders are tasked with supporting reforms that teachers feel are unnecessary. Teachers may believe their current curriculum is good enough and may not have the motivation to make changes. At the heart of effective instructional leadership are strong, trusting relationships. We recognize that both leaders and teachers may need support and encouragement from district-level leaders, and it may take time for teachers to understand why reform is needed. Thankfully, both motivation and trust can be developed by engaging in low-risk activities together. An important way to begin is by encouraging teachers to try out new strategies while the leader provides motivational and helpful feedback that is purely formative (i.e., without evaluative implications). Learning alongside teachers and engaging collaboratively in efforts to integrate the science practices can also help foster trust and enthusiasm about the practices.

Taken together, these challenges can present barriers to the implementation of the science practices, but they are not insurmountable. With proper support from district leaders, time for professional learning, and the kinds of tools we share in this book, both teachers and leaders can develop the skills and understanding to integrate the science practices fully into their classrooms. This process will certainly take time and focus, but we know it is possible and a worthwhile endeavor.

Moving Forward

Implementing the science practices is certainly a challenge—as is the first step of taking up the resources and tools outlined in this book. Nevertheless, we are confident that moving ahead one step at a time will lead to improved science instruction for all students. To this end, planning a schoolwide strategy in advance will help ensure success. What follows are a few potential pathways to initiate this work in your school.

One option is to take an individualized approach to implementation. By introducing the tools as part of the supervision cycle, leaders can begin this work with individual teachers, identifying where they fall on the continuum and the differentiated support they may need to move ahead. This also allows leaders to personally identify a few teachers who become relative experts in the practices and can serve as important partners in the work of expanding implementation to other teachers.

Another approach engages the entire school. This schoolwide approach starts with faculty training to give teachers an introduction to the science practices and tools before engaging with them in the supervision cycle. Leaders can encourage the faculty to help identify which specific practices make the most sense to begin with and help develop a plan for how to collectively engage in using the tools, such as peer observation and collaborative lesson planning.

A third approach focuses on the district level. If your school district is in the process of adopting a new science curriculum and you are at the stage of identifying curriculum, your knowledge of the science practices may help inform decisions about which curriculum to implement. Leaders may want to collaborate with the curriculum director(s) to identify a new science curriculum or set of curricula to adopt. By partnering with the district, your school may have a chance to implement the science practices as you integrate that new curriculum. As you approach this shift in curriculum, leverage the tools from this book to help teachers understand and enact the shifts in the new curriculum, rather than mapping them to instructional practices they've used in the past.

Whichever approach makes sense in your context, we know you will find a variety of uses for the tools we have shared. We designed them with the idea that your context will shape how you choose to implement the science practices and the ways you use the tools. We look forward to seeing the different approaches you take to the materials as you adapt them to meet a variety of purposes. Anchoring your instructional leadership in trusting relationships, formative opportunities for reflection, and subject-specific insights will lead to the effective implementation of the science practices—one step at a time.

Appendix A

Science Practices Continuum: Supervision

This continuum is intended for teachers and administrators to use in guiding and monitoring science practice–based instruction. The levels reflect increasingly sophisticated instruction of the practices and are not grade-level specific; teachers can teach in developmentally appropriate ways at any of these levels. Appendix F in the NGSS provides significantly more detail for each practice (which should be integrated as both students and teachers develop greater fluency with each practice). The practices are grouped into the "Investigating," "Sensemaking," and "Critiquing" practices.

	Level 1	Level 2	Level 3	Level 4
1. Asking Questions	Teacher does not provide opportunities for students to ask questions.	Teacher provides opportunities for students to ask questions. Students' questions are both scientific and non-scientific (i.e., not answerable through the gathering of evidence about natural phenomena).	Teacher provides opportunities for students to ask *scientific* questions to investigate natural phenomena. Students do not *evaluate* the merits and limitations of the questions.	Teacher provides opportunities for students to ask *scientific* questions to investigate natural phenomena. Students *evaluate* the merits and limitations of the questions.
3. Planning and Carrying Out Investigations	Teacher does not provide opportunities for students to design or conduct investigations.	Teacher provides opportunities for students to conduct investigations to confirm ideas they have learned about, and these opportunities are typically teacher-driven. Students do not make decisions about experimental variables or investigational methods (e.g., number of trials).	Teacher provides opportunities for students to *design or conduct* investigations to gather data to figure out how or why a natural phenomenon occurs. Students *make decisions about experimental variables, controls, and investigational methods.*	Teacher provides opportunities for students to *design and conduct* investigations to gather data to figure out how or why a natural phenomenon occurs. Students *make decisions about experimental variables, controls, and investigational methods.*
5. Using Mathematics and Computational Thinking	Teacher does not provide opportunities for students to use mathematical skills (i.e., measuring, comparing, estimating) or concepts (i.e., ratios).	Teacher provides opportunities for students to use mathematical skills or concepts to confirm science ideas they have learned about. These are *not connected to answering scientific questions.*	Teacher provides opportunities for students to use mathematical skills or concepts that are connected to *answering scientific questions concerning figuring out natural phenomena.*	Teacher provides opportunities for students to *make decisions about what* mathematical skills or concepts to use. Students use mathematical skills or concepts to answer scientific questions concerning figuring out natural phenomena.

Investigating Practices

2. Developing and Using Models	Teacher does not provide opportunities for students to create or use models.	Teacher provides opportunities for students to create or use models. The models focus on *describing science ideas or natural phenomena.* Students do not *evaluate* the merits and limitations of the model.	Teacher provides opportunities for students to create or use models focused on *predicting or explaining* natural phenomena. Students *do not evaluate* the merits and limitations of the model.	Teacher provides opportunities for students to create or use models focused on *predicting or explaining* natural phenomena. Students *do evaluate* the merits and limitations of the model.
4. Analyzing and Interpreting Data	Teacher does not provide opportunities for students to analyze data. Students may record data but do not analyze it.	Teacher provides opportunities for students to work with data, which could include organizing or grouping the data. These opportunities support students to *recognize patterns or relationships* that confirm science ideas they have learned about.	Teacher provides opportunities for students to work with data to organize or group the data in a table or graph. These opportunities support students to *recognize patterns or relationships in data to figure out natural phenomena.*	Teacher provides opportunities for students to *make decisions about how to* analyze data (e.g., table or graph) and work with the data to create the representation. These opportunities support students to *recognize patterns or relationships in data to figure out natural phenomena.*
6. Constructing Explanations	Teacher does not provide opportunities for students to create scientific explanations.	Teacher provides opportunities for students to construct scientific explanations that are *descriptive* instead of explaining how or why a natural phenomenon occurs. Students *do not use appropriate evidence* to support their explanations.	Teacher provides opportunities for students to construct scientific explanations that are *descriptive* instead of explaining how or why a natural phenomenon occurs. Students *use appropriate evidence to* support their explanations.	Teacher provides opportunities for students to construct scientific explanations that focus on explaining how or why a natural phenomenon occurs. Students *use appropriate evidence to* support their explanations.

Sensemaking Practices

(continued)

		Level 1	Level 2	Level 3	Level 4
Critiquing Practices	**7. Engaging in Argument from Evidence**	Teacher does not provide opportunities for students to engage in argumentation.	Teacher provides opportunities for students to engage in argumentation where they support their claims about science ideas with evidence or reasoning, but the discourse is primarily *teacher-driven*, or there are not competing arguments for students to make (i.e., not two or more potential claims for students to argue about).	Teacher provides opportunities for *student-driven argumentation* where students support their competing claims about natural phenomena with evidence and reasoning. Students agree and disagree, but rarely engage in critique.	Teacher provides opportunities for *student-driven argumentation* where students support their competing claims about natural phenomena with evidence and reasoning. Students critique competing claims during which they build on and question one another's ideas.
	8. Obtaining, Evaluating, and Communicating Information	Teacher does not provide opportunities for students to read text for scientific information.	Teacher provides opportunities for students to read text to *obtain scientific information about science ideas, but they do not evaluate this information*. Students also do not compare or combine information from multiple texts considering the strengths of the information and sources.	Teacher provides opportunities for students to *read and evaluate text to obtain scientific information to figure out natural phenomena. Students do not compare or combine information* from multiple texts considering the strengths of the information and sources.	Teacher provides opportunities for students to *read and evaluate text to obtain scientific information to figure out natural phenomena. Students compare and combine information* from multiple texts considering the strengths of the information and sources.

Instructional Elements for the Science Practices

Learning about --Figuring out

Grounded in natural phenomena   Focused on scientific evidence   Student-directed and collaborative   Informed by critique

Science Practices Continuum: Instruction

This continuum is intended for teachers and administrators to use in guiding and evaluating student performance in the science practices. The levels reflect increasingly sophisticated engagement in the practices and are not grade-level specific; students can engage in the practices in developmentally appropriate ways at any of these levels. Appendix F in the NGSS provides significantly more detail for each practice (which should be integrated as both students and teachers develop greater fluency with each practice). The practices are grouped into the "Investigating," "Sensemaking," and "Critiquing" practices.

		Level 1	Level 2	Level 3	Level 4
Investigating Practices	**1. Asking Questions**	Students do not ask questions.	Students ask questions. Students' questions are both *scientific and non-scientific* (i.e., not answerable through the gathering of evidence about natural phenomena).	Students' ask *scientific questions to investigate natural phenomena*. Students *do not evaluate* the merits and limitations of the questions for investigating phenomena.	Students' ask *scientific questions to investigate natural phenomena*. Students evaluate the merits and limitations of the questions for investigating phenomena.
	3. Planning and Carrying Out Investigations	Students do not design or conduct investigations.	Students conduct investigations to gather data to confirm science ideas they have learned about. These opportunities are typically *teacher-driven. Students do not make decisions about* experimental variables or investigational methods.	Students *design or conduct investigations to gather data to figure out how or why a natural phenomenon occurs. Students make decisions about* experimental variables, controls, or investigational methods.	Students *design and conduct investigations to gather data to figure out how or why a natural phenomenon occurs. Students make decisions about* experimental variables, controls, and investigational methods.
	5. Using Mathematics and Computational Thinking	Students do not use mathematical skills (i.e., measuring, estimating) or concepts (i.e., ratios).	Students use mathematical skills or concepts to confirm science ideas they have already learned about. These are *not connected to answering scientific questions.*	Students use mathematical skills or concepts to *answer scientific questions concerning figuring out natural phenomena.*	Students *make decisions* about what mathematical skills or concepts to use. Students use mathematical skills or concepts to *answer scientific questions concerning figuring out natural phenomena.*

Sensemaking Practices				
2. **Developing and Using Models**	Students do not create or use models.	Students create or use models focused on *describing science ideas or natural phenomena.* Students *do not evaluate* the merits and limitations of the model.	Students create or use models focused on *pre-dicting or explaining natural phenomena. Students do not evaluate* the merits and limitations of the model.	Students create or use models focused on *pre-dicting or explaining natural phenomena. Students evaluate* the merits and limitations of the model.
4. **Analyzing and Interpreting Data**	Students may record data but do not analyze data.	Students work with data to organize or group the data in a table or graph. Stu-dents recognize patterns or relationships in data to confirm science ideas they *have already learned about.*	Students work with data to organize or group the data in a table or graph. Students recognize pat-terns or relationships in data *to figure out natural phenomena.*	Students *make decisions about how to analyze* data (e.g., table or graph) and work with the data to create the representa-tion. Students recognize patterns or relationships *to figure out natural phenomena.*
6. **Constructing Explanations**	Students do not create scientific explanations.	Students attempt to create scientific explanations, but students' explanations are *descriptive* instead of explaining *how or why a natural phenomenon occurs.* Students *do not use appropriate evidence to support their explanations.*	Students attempt to create scientific explanations, but students' explanations are *descriptive* instead of explaining *how or why a natural phenomenon* occurs. Students *use appropriate evidence to support their explanations.*	Students construct expla-nations that focus on explaining *how or why a natural phenomenon occurs and use appropriate evidence to support their explanations.*

(continued)

		Level 1	Level 2	Level 3	Level 4
Critiquing Practices	**7. Engaging in Argument from Evidence**	Students do not engage in argumentation	Students engage in argumentation where they support their *claims with evidence or reasoning*, but the discourse is primarily *teacher-driven*, or there are not competing arguments for students to make (i.e., not two or more potential claims for students to argue about).	Students engage in *student-driven argumentation*. Students *support their competing claims about natural phenomena* with *evidence and reasoning*. Students *agree and disagree*, but rarely engage in critique.	Students engage in *student-driven argumentation*. Students *support their competing claims about natural phenomena* with *evidence and reasoning*. Students *critique* competing claims during which they build on and question one another's ideas.
	8. Obtaining, Evaluating, and Communicating Information	Students do not read text for scientific information.	Students read text to *obtain* scientific information to about science ideas, but they do *not evaluate* this information. Students also *do not compare or combine information* from multiple texts considering the strengths of the information and sources.	Students *read and evaluate text to obtain scientific information to figure out natural phenomena*. Students *do not compare or combine information* from multiple texts considering the strengths of the information and sources.	Students *read and evaluate text to obtain scientific information to figure out natural phenomena*. Students *compare and combine information* from multiple texts considering the strengths of the information and sources.

Instructional Elements for Science Practices

Learning about --Figuring out

Grounded in natural phenomena | Focused on scientific evidence | Student-directed and collaborative | Informed by critique

Appendix B

Science Instruction Observation Form

Educator Name: Supervisor Name:

Observation Date: Observation Time/Duration:

Intended Observation Focus:

NGSS Practices		
Which practices are observed?		
Investigation Practices	*Sensemaking Practices*	*Critiquing Practices*
☐ 1. Asking Questions	☐ 2. Developing and Using Models	☐ 7. Engaging in Argument from Evidence
☐ 3. Planning and Carrying Out Investigations	☐ 4. Analyzing and Interpreting Data	☐ 8. Obtaining, Evaluating, and Communicating Information
☐ 5. Using Mathematics and Computational Thinking	☐ 6. Constructing Explanations	
Observation Evidence		
What are the educator and students saying and doing?		

NGSS Practices Progression
Where do the observed practices fall along the progression?
Practice #: 1 2 3 4 5 6 7 8   1------------------------2------------------------3------------------------4
Practice #: 1 2 3 4 5 6 7 8   1------------------------2------------------------3------------------------4
Practice #: 1 2 3 4 5 6 7 8   1------------------------2------------------------3------------------------4
Rationale for Levels   *What determined the ratings of practices?*

Appendix C

Instructional Strategies: Asking Questions

Scientific questions lead to explanations of how the natural world works and can be empirically tested using evidence.

Potential Instructional Strategies for *Asking Questions*
1. Ask students to share ideas of scientific questions about a specific topic. Emphasize that scientific questions should be questions that can be answered using data from investigations.
2. Provide examples and nonexamples of scientific questions. Ask students to work in groups to sort the questions.
3. Model the writing of scientific questions. Demonstrate that since scientific questions can be answered using data from investigations, the question should contain two variables.
4. Provide fill-in-the-blank questions for students. (e.g., How does the _____ affect _____?)
5. Have students identify the variables in scientific questions (e.g., underline the independent variable, circle the dependent variable). Scaffold, if necessary, by doing several as a whole class and then having students practice with their own (or peers') scientific questions.
6. Provide opportunities for students to work together to write scientific questions that will be used for in-class investigations. Encourage students to critique one another's ideas and pose questions to one another as part of the discussion.
7. Have students ask scientific questions they have about a demonstrated phenomenon. Remind students that scientific questions are answerable by doing experiments.
8. Ask students to explain how they would go about answering a scientific question.

For a classroom example of instruction using this science practice, visit www.sciencepracticesleadership.com/example-lessons and click on the Grade 2 Exemplar under Case Studies.

Instructional Strategies: Developing and Using Models

A *model*, which is an abstract representation of a phenomenon, is a tool used to predict or explain the natural world. Models can be represented as diagrams, 3D objects, mathematical representations, analogies, or computer simulations.

Potential Instructional Strategies for *Developing and Using Models*
1. Have students work in groups to create models of nonobservable phenomena (e.g., lunar cycles, erosion). Be explicit that models offer explanatory accounts; they show how or why a phenomenon occurs.
2. Show students an example of a scientific model and a nonexample, such as a labeled diagram. Have students compare and contrast the two. Highlight that the scientific model shows how a phenomenon occurs, whereas the labeled diagram does not.
3. Provide opportunities for students to make decisions about the type of model they will create, such as a picture, physical creation, or computer animation. Emphasize that there is no one "right" way to create a model. Rather, models should show how or why the phenomenon under study occurs.
4. Provide graphic organizers to support students in planning their models. Sections of the graphic organizer might include "key ideas" and room to sketch the model. At the end of the graphic organizer, provide a checklist so students can be sure their proposed model shows how or why the phenomenon occurs and is not only descriptive.
5. Provide a range of materials and computer access so students can choose the type of model to create. Before students select their medium, facilitate a discussion about the benefits and drawbacks of each.
6. Have students do a "gallery walk" of the different models they create. Provide students with a chart to make notes about how the various models do and do not explain the phenomenon being modeled. Give students sticky notes to post suggestions and comments for their peers.
7. Ask students to critique models from various sources, such as texts, the internet, and physical representations in the classroom. Facilitate a discussion of the benefits and drawbacks of the different models. Emphasize that all models have benefits and drawbacks.
8. Ask students to apply a model to a different example and then revise the model to reflect the new information (e.g., apply a model for sinking and floating of objects to the floating of a boat).

For a classroom example of instruction using this science practice, visit www.sciencepracticesleadership.com/example-lessons and click on the Grade 7 Exemplar under Case Studies.

Instructional Strategies: Planning and Carrying Out Investigations

An *investigation* is a systematic way to gather data (e.g., observations or measurements) about the natural world, either in the field or in a laboratory setting.

Potential Instructional Strategies for *Planning and Carrying Out Investigations*
1. Put students in small groups to complete investigations. Assign each student a job to do. Model the job responsibilities before beginning so students understand what is expected of them while performing the investigation.
2. Assign groups to specific spaces in the classroom to conduct their investigations. This helps ensure each group has sufficient space to conduct the investigation and that the groups will not disturb one another.
3. Give students sticky notes to label materials in an investigation. This can help younger students or students who struggle with writing to show the outcome of an investigation without the demands of recording in a data table.
4. Have students vote on their prediction for the outcome of an experiment. Record predictions on the board. Ask students to revisit their predictions after they have gathered data.
5. Provide a scientific question and have groups of students design an investigation to answer the question. Provide students with a graphic organizer to record the variables (independent, dependent, constants), procedure, materials, and data table.
6. Show students several procedures for investigations that have varying numbers of trials, materials, or types of data tables. Ask students to critique the procedures based on the scientific question being explored.
7. Show students several procedures for investigations in which one student only changes one variable while the others alter multiple variables at the same time. Ask students to critique the procedures to discuss the idea of a fair test and only changing one variable at a time.
8. Provide a choice of three or four scientific questions to explore about a specific topic. Have small groups of students select their question and design and carry out an investigation to answer that question.
9. Provide a general experimental procedure but allow student choice in terms of variables to be manipulated (e.g., materials to test, length of time).

For classroom examples of instruction using this science practice, visit www.sciencepracticesleadership.com/example-lessons and click on the Grade 2 Exemplar and Grade 5 Exemplar under Case Studies.

Instructional Strategies: Analyzing and Interpreting Data

Analyzing and Interpreting Data includes making sense of the data produced during investigations. Because patterns are not always obvious, this includes using a range of tools, such as tables, graphs, and other visualization techniques.

Potential Instructional Strategies for *Analyzing and Interpreting Data*

1. After an investigation, ask each group of students to briefly state a pattern they see in the data. Provide sentence starters, such as "As the amount of _____ increases…" and "We saw that changing _____ caused…"

2. Provide written steps for students to follow to scaffold analyzing complex data tables. For example, students might be asked to first state how many trials were conducted, then asked what pattern they see in the first column of the data table. As students' ability with finding the patterns in data improves through the school year, slowly remove the scaffold.

3. Ask students to vote (thumbs up/thumbs down) whether or not they agree with a fellow student's interpretation of the patterns in data.

4. To practice figuring out patterns in the data, give groups of students a data table and sentence strips with various statements about patterns in the data. Have students decide whether each statement is accurate or inaccurate based on the data table.

5. Have groups of students compare and contrast their data tables. If differences exist in the data, ask students to hypothesize about why these differences exist. Have students make a plan to reduce sources of error in future iterations of the investigation (e.g., dropping a ball from the same height, having the same students operate a stopwatch through the investigation).

6. Ask students to graph their data to visually represent patterns in the data. Provide checklists for students to use to ensure their graphs contain key components, such as labels on the axes and a title.

7. Conduct a gallery walk for students to view and critique one another's data tables or graphs. Encourage students to use sticky notes to ask questions and provide feedback about how well their data tables show the patterns in the data. Give students time to use the feedback to improve their work.

8. Model for students how to construct a graph. Talk about what decisions must be made when creating a graph (e.g., bar graph vs. line graph) and the reasons for one choice or another. Point out aspects of graphs that enable others to comprehend patterns in the graph (e.g., reasonable intervals on the axes).

9. Hang posters in the classroom with examples of different types of graphs (e.g., bar, line) students can reference as they decide what type of graph to construct and as they make their graphs.

10. After students construct a graph for the data, ask them to defend their choice. Facilitate a discussion about the differences in how each graph type shows the patterns in the data.

11. Have students write one or two sentences that summarize the pattern(s) in a graph. Provide sentence starters, such as "My graph shows…" and "Over time, plant A…"

For a classroom example of instruction using this science practice, visit www.sciencepracticesleadership.com/example-lessons and click on the Grade 5 Exemplar under Case Studies.

Instructional Strategies: Using Mathematics and Computational Thinking

Mathematical and computational thinking involves using tools and mathematical concepts to address a scientific question.

Potential Instructional Strategies for *Using Computational and Mathematical Thinking*
1. Provide opportunities for students to perform calculations on their gathered data, such as finding the mean (average) of several trials of data.
2. Engage older students in using computer programs, such as Microsoft Excel, to analyze large data sets from a scientific organization (e.g., NASA, NOAA).
3. Create activities in which students are given a scientific question and must decide how to use mathematical or computational thinking to address the question.
4. Use various tools to gather data, such as graduated cylinders, thermometers, and balances.
5. Have older students decide whether to represent their data in different ways, such as using ratios or percentages.
6. Engage students in investigations that require them to use mathematical operations (e.g., subtract quantities to determine the volume of an object).

For a classroom example of instruction using this science practice, visit www.sciencepracticesleadership.com/example-lessons and click on the Grade 2 Exemplar under Case Studies.

Instructional Strategies: Constructing Explanations

A *scientific explanation* is an explanatory account that articulates how or why a natural phenomenon occurs and how it is supported by evidence and scientific ideas.

Potential Instructional Strategies for *Constructing Explanations*
1. Discuss key features of explanations in science: explanatory accounts, science ideas, and evidence. An explanatory account describes how or why a phenomenon occurs. Science ideas are key concepts or principles students apply to make sense of a specific phenomenon (e.g., an example). Evidence is scientific data, such as measurements and observations.
2. Create a poster with the key features for a scientific explanation that shows how or why something occurs.
3. Revise explanation questions to ensure that students need to answer with more than a simple "yes" or "no"; rather, they require an explanatory account.
4. Provide both strong and weak examples (e.g., describe a phenomenon instead of explaining it). Critique the examples as a class.
5. Provide students with scaffolds, such as sentence starters, questions, or graphic organizers, that highlight the key features. For example, a graphic organizer could include three sections labeled (1) Your explanation: How or why?, (2) Big science ideas that support your explanation, and (3) Evidence that supports your explanation.
6. Ask students to highlight the key features of an explanation (explanatory account, science ideas, and evidence) in their own or a peer's writing.
7. Ask students to give feedback to one another about written explanations. Provide sentence starters to help students make specific statements about the explanations. Examples of sentences starters can include "I have a question about your evidence," "I am not sure your writing explains why _____ occurs. Can you explain that to me?" and "How can we use our big science ideas to help explain _____?"

For a classroom example of instruction using this science practice, visit www.sciencepracticesleadership.com/example-lessons and click on the Grade 5 Exemplar under Case Studies.

Instructional Strategies: Engaging in Argument from Evidence

Scientific argumentation is a process that occurs when there are multiple ideas or claims (e.g., explanations, models) to discuss and reconcile. An argument includes a claim supported by evidence and reasoning as well as evaluating and critiquing competing arguments.

Potential Instructional Strategies for *Engaging in Argument from Evidence*

1. Introduce students to the argumentation framework of claim, evidence, and reasoning (CER). A claim answers a question or problem, which could be an explanation or model. Evidence is data that support the claim, such as observations and measurements. Reasoning explains why the evidence supports the claim using scientific ideas or principles.

2. Provide students with scaffolds, such as a graphic organizer, sentence starters, or questions that highlight the CER components to help them craft their arguments.

3. Revise argumentation questions to ensure there is more than one possible claim that students could potentially support with evidence. When students have multiple competing claims, there is more opportunity for critique.

4. Facilitate a discussion about the norms for argumentation. Explain to students that they should be talking directly to one another and not through the teacher. In addition, they should be questioning and critiquing one another's ideas. However, it is also important for students to be willing to change their minds if new ideas or evidence are presented by their peers that convince them of the strength of a competing claim.

5. Create a poster in the classroom that supports the CER structure, as well as students critiquing different ideas. It could include sentence starters (e.g., My evidence is…, I disagree because…) or questions (e.g., What are some other possible claims? Do we have support for those claims? Why did you decide to use that evidence to support your claim? Could the data be interpreted in a different way?).

6. Model for students what it looks like to question or critique another person's idea. For example, "I disagree with Maria's claim because I interpreted the data in a different way. I think the data show that lung capacity is important for…"

7. Limit teacher talk during argumentation by physically removing yourself from the discussion (e.g., sit in the corner of the room) and/or telling students that you have a specific task during the discussion. For example, you can tell the class that your job is to record the different evidence that comes up during the conversation and that you will not be actively talking during the discussion.

For a classroom example of instruction using this science practice, visit www.sciencepracticesleadership.com/example-lessons and click on the Grade 7 Exemplar under Case Studies.

Instructional Strategies: Obtaining, Evaluating, and Communicating Information

Obtaining, evaluating, and communicating information occur through reading and writing texts as well as communicating orally. Scientific information needs to be critically evaluated and persuasively communicated as it supports the engagement in the other science practices.

Potential Instructional Strategies for
Obtaining, Evaluating, and Communicating Information

1. Have students read a text in small groups that contains evidence and science ideas about a specific topic. Ask students to underline the evidence and put a star next to the science ideas.

2. Explicitly remind students of the definition of *scientific evidence* (measurements and observations). Create a poster with this definition for students to reference in the classroom.

3. Provide students with two or more texts on the same topic. Ask students to compare and contrast the texts, focusing on how well the authors defend their claims. Have students decide which is the most persuasive text. Tell students they will need to explain why they think that text is most persuasive.

4. Do a jigsaw activity with multiple texts. Put students into groups and give each group a different text on a related topic. When students have read the text, mix up the groups so one person who has read each text is in each group. Ask students to briefly summarize their text for their group.

5. Develop a checklist of questions students can ask as they evaluate texts. For example, Does the text have a clear claim? Does the text use scientific evidence to support the claim? Does the text have enough scientific evidence to support the claim?

6. Watch two short videos (or listen to two podcasts) about a similar topic. Ask students to compare and contrast the different perspectives on the same topic (e.g., genetically modified food).

For a classroom example of instruction using this science practice, visit www.sciencepracticesleadership.com/example-lessons and click on the Grade 7 Exemplar under Case Studies.

References

Allen, C. D., & Penuel, W. R. (2015). Studying teachers' sensemaking to investigate teachers' responses to professional development focused on new standards. *Journal of Teacher Education, 66*(2), 136–149.

Bambrick-Santoyo, P. (2012). *Leverage leadership: A practical guide to building exceptional schools.* San Francisco: Jossey-Bass.

Bang, M., Brown, B., Calabrese Barton, A., Rosebery, A., & Warren, B. (2017). Towards more equitable learning in science: Expanding relationships among students, teachers, and science practices. In C. V. Schwarz, C. Passmore, & B. J. Reiser (Eds.), *Helping students make sense of the world using next generation science and engineering practices* (pp. 33–58). Arlington, VA: NSTA Press.

Bell, P., Bricker, L., Tzou, C., Lee, T., & Van Horne, K. (2012). Exploring the science framework: Engaging learners in scientific practices related to obtaining, evaluating, and communicating information. *Science Scope, 36*(3), 17.

Bredeson, P. V. (2003). *Designs for learning: A new architecture for professional development in schools.* Thousand Oaks, CA: Corwin.

Brown, B. A. (2019). *Science in the city: Culturally relevant STEM education.* Cambridge, MA: Harvard Education Press.

Cherbow, K., McNeill, K., Lowenhaupt, R., McKinley, M., & Lowell, B. (2019). NGSS lesson adaptations: A resource for integrating the science practices into your instruction. *Science and Children: 56*(5), 73–77.

Cheuk, T. (2013). *Relationships and convergences among the mathematics, science, and ELA practices.* Refined version of diagram created by the Understanding Language Initiative for ELP Standards. Palo Alto, CA: Stanford University. Available at: https://ell.stanford.edu/sites/default/files/VennDiagram_practices_v11%208-30-13%20color.pdf

Coburn, C. E. (2001). Collective sensemaking about reading: How teachers mediate reading policy in their professional communities. *Educational Evaluation and Policy Analysis, 23*(2), 145–170.

Coburn, C. E. (2006). Framing the problem of reading instruction: Using frame analysis to uncover the microprocesses of policy implementation. *American Educational Research Journal, 43*(3), 343–349.

Cohen, D. K. (1990). A revolution in one classroom: The case of Mrs. Oublier. *Educational Evaluation and Policy Analysis, 12*(3), 311–329.

Cunningham, C. M. (2017). Engineering practices. In C. V. Schwarz, C. Passmore, & B. J. Reiser (Eds.), *Helping students make sense of the world using next generation science and engineering practices* (pp. 283–307). Arlington, VA: NSTA Press.

Curry, M. (2008). Critical friends groups: The possibilities and limitations embedded in teacher professional communities aimed at instructional improvement and school reform. *Teachers College Record, 110*(4), 733–774.

Danielson, C. (2007). *Enhancing professional practice: A framework for teaching* (2nd ed.). Alexandria, VA: ASCD.

Desimone, L. M. (2009). Improving impact studies of teachers' professional development: Toward better conceptualizations and measures. *Educational Researcher, 38*(3), 181–199.

Donaldson, M. L. (2009). *So long, Lake Wobegon? Using teacher evaluation to raise teacher quality.* Washington, DC: Center for American Progress.

DuFour, R., & Eaker, R. (2009). *Professional learning communities at work: Best practices for enhancing students achievement.* Bloomington, IN: Solution Tree.

Engineering Is Elementary. (2011). Engineering is elementary, 2nd edition [website]. Retrieved from www.eie.org/stem-curricula/engineering-grades-prek-8/engineering-is-elementary

Echevarria, J., Vogt, M., & Short, D. (2016). *Making content comprehensible for English learners: The SIOP model* (5th ed.). New York: Pearson.

Geier, R., Blumenfeld, P. C., Marx, R. W., Krajcik, J. S., Fishman, B., Soloway, E., & Clay-Chambers, J. (2008). Standardized test outcomes for students engaged in inquiry-based science curricula in the context of urban reform. *Journal of Research in Science Teaching, 45*(8), 922–939.

Glickman, C. D. (2002). *Leadership for learning: How to help teachers succeed.* Alexandria, VA: ASCD.

Halverson, R., Feinstein, N. R., & Meshoulam, D. (2011). School leadership for science education. In G. E. DeBoer (Ed.), *The role of public policy in K–12 science education* (pp. 397–430). Charlotte, NC: Information Age Publishing.

Harris, C. J., Penuel, W. R., D'Angelo, C. M., DeBarger, A. H., Gallagher, L. P., Kennedy, C. A., Cheng, B. H., & Krajcik, J. S. (2015). Impact of project-based curriculum materials on student learning in science: Results of a randomized controlled trial. *Journal of Research in Science Teaching, 52*(10), 1362–1385.

Hill, H., & Grossman, P. (2013). Learning from teacher observations: Challenges and opportunities posed by new teacher evaluation systems. *Harvard Educational Review, 83*(2), 371–384.

Jackson, R. R. (2013). *Never underestimate your teachers: Instructional leadership for excellence in every classroom.* Alexandria, VA: ASCD.

Kennedy, M. M. (2016). How does professional development improve teaching? *Review of Educational Research, 86*(4), 945–980.

Knight, J. (2008). *Coaching: Approaches and perspectives.* Thousand Oaks, CA: Corwin.

Kraft, M. A., & Gilmour, A. F. (2016). Can principals promote teacher development as evaluators? A case study of principals' views and experiences. *Educational Administration Quarterly, 52*(5), 711–753.

Lehrer, R., & Schauble, L. (2006). Scientific thinking and science literacy. In W. Damon & R. M. Lerner (Eds.), *Handbook of child psychology* (4th ed., pp. 153–196). Hoboken, NJ: Wiley.

Lowell, B. R., & McNeill, K. L. (2019). Keeping critical thinking afloat: Shifting from activity-based to phenomenon-based planning. *Science Scope, 43*(1), 64–69.

Lowenhaupt, R., & McNeill, K. L. (2019). Subject-specific instructional leadership in K8 schools: The supervision of science in an era of reform. *Leadership and Policy in Schools*, *18*(3), 460–484.

Marshall, K. (2013). *Rethinking teacher supervision and evaluation: How to work smart, build collaboration, and close the achievement gap.* Hoboken, NJ: Wiley.

McNeill, K. L., Katsh-Singer, R., & Pelletier, P. (2015). Assessing science practices: Moving your class along a continuum. *Science Scope*, *39*(4), 21–28.

McNeill, K. L., Lowenhaupt, R. J., & Katsh-Singer, R. (2018). Instructional leadership in the era of the NGSS: Principals' understandings of science practices. *Science Education*, *102*(3), 452–473.

Myung, J., & Martinez, K. (2013). *Strategies for enhancing the impact of post-observation feedback for teachers.* Princeton, NJ: Carnegie Foundation for the Advancement of Teaching.

NGSS Lead States. (2013). *Next Generation Science Standards: For states, by states.* Washington, DC: National Academies Press.

National Research Council. (2012). *A framework for K–12 science education: Practices, crosscutting concepts, and core ideas.* Washington, DC: National Academies Press.

National Research Council. (2015). *Guide to implementing the next generation science standards.* Washington, DC: National Academies Press.

Nelson, B. S., & Sassi, A. (2005). *The effective principal: Instructional leadership for high-quality learning.* New York: Teachers College Press.

Osborne, J. (2010). Arguing to learn in science: The role of collaborative, critical discourse. *Science*, *328*(5977), 463–466.

Rigby, J. G., Larbi-Cherif, A., Rosenquist, B. A., Sharpe, C. J., Cobb, P., & Smith, T. (2017). Administrator observation and feedback: Does it lead toward improvement in inquiry-oriented math instruction? *Educational Administration Quarterly*, *53*(3), 475–516.

Schwarz, C. V., Passmore, C., & Reiser, B. J. (2017). Moving beyond "knowing about" science to making sense of the natural world. In C. V. Schwarz, C. Passmore, & B. J. Reiser (Eds.), *Helping students make sense of the world using next generation science and engineering practices* (pp. 3–21). Arlington, VA: NSTA Press.

Sergiovanni, T. J., Starratt, R. J., & Cho, V. (2014). *Supervision: A redefinition* (9th ed.). New York: McGraw-Hill.

Sherin, M. G., & van Es, E. A. (2005). Using video to support teachers' ability to notice classroom interactions. *Journal of Technology and Teacher Education*, *13*(3), 475–491.

Shulman, L. S. (1986). Those who understand: Knowledge growth in teaching. *Educational Researcher*, *15*(2), 4–14.

Spillane, J. P. (2005). Primary school leadership practice: How the subject matters. *School Leadership & Management*, *25*(4), 383–397.

Spillane, J. P. (2009). *Standards deviation: How schools misunderstand education policy.* Cambridge, MA: Harvard University Press.

Stein, M. K., & Nelson, B. S. (2003). Leadership content knowledge. *Educational Evaluation and Policy Analysis*, *25*(4), 423–448.

Wiggins, G. (2012). Seven keys to effective feedback. *Educational Leadership*, *70*(1), 10–16.

Index

The letter *f* following a page locator denotes a figure.

Analyzing and Interpreting Data. *See* Data, Analyzing and Interpreting

Argument, Engaging in from Evidence. *See* Evidence, Engaging in Argument from

Asking Questions. *See* Questions, Asking

collaboration
    in implementing observation, 72
    in implementing supervision, 54–55

Computatiional Thinking, Using Mathematics and. *See* Mathematics and Computational Thinking, Using

Constructing Explanations. *See* Explanations, Constructing

critiquing practices. *See also individual practices*
    in the Continuum, 30*f*
    focus of, 21
    individual practices in, 16*f*
    vignette, 21–23

cross-discipline practices, 12–14

curriculum and instruction, using groups to analyze, 23

Data, Analyzing and Interpreting
    defined, 13*f*
    instructional strategies, 128–129
    lesson adaptations, 103, 103–104*f*
    vignette, 19–21

Developing and Using Models. *See* Models, Developing and Using

Engaging in Argument from Evidence. *See* Evidence, Engaging in Argument from

equity, science practices and, 14–15

evaluation, rubrics for, 46

evaluation framework, theorizing the need for a science-specific, 28–29

evidence, building and critiquing ideas using, 31

Evidence, Engaging in Argument from
    defined, 13*f*
    key levers, 37–39, 38*f*
    vignette, 21–23

experts, using existing for PD, 105

Explanations, Constructing
    defined, 13*f*
    instructional strategies, 131
    vignette, 19–21

feedback
    in instructional growth, 76–77
    key levers, using, 78, 82*f*
    science-specific, NGSS requirement for, 28
    in the supervision cycle, 45*f*, 49
    vignette, 75–76, 90

feedback strategies
    focus on one practice, 78, 82*f*
    follow-ups, 89–90
    plan for the future, 78–79, 82*f*
    praise, 77–78, 82*f*
    probing questions, 78, 82*f*
    recommended, 78–79, 82*f*

feedback strategies—(*continued*)
   specificity, 78, 82*f*
   use the language of the continuum, 89
   using flexibly, 88–89
feedback tools
   Instructional Strategies Tool, 79,
      125–132
   Post-Observation Conference Work-
      sheet, 77–79, 82*f*, 88–89
   practice example, 79–88
follow-ups in feedback, 89–90

goal setting in the supervision cycle, 52–53

Information, Obtaining, Evaluating and
   Communicating
   defined, 13*f*
   vignette, 21–23
instructional growth, feedback in, 76–77
instructional leaders, 28
Instructional Leadership for Science Practices (ILSP) project, 3–7
instructional reform, requirements for, 6
instruction in the Continuum, 29–32
investigating practices. *See also individual
   practices*
   in the Continuum, 30*f*
   focus of, 17
   individual practices in, 16*f*
   vignette, 17–19
Investigations, Planning and Carrying Out
   defined, 13*f*
   instructional strategies, 127
   key levers, 34–36, 35*f*
   vignette, 17–19

leadership, subject-specific, 28
leadership content knowledge (LCK), 6

Mathematics and Computational Thinking, Using
   defined, 13*f*
   instructional strategies, 130
   vignette, 17–19

mistakes, allowing for, 54
Models, Developing and Using
   defined, 13*f*
   example of, 12
   instructional strategies, 126
   key levers, 36–37, 36*f*
   vignette, 19–21

natural phenomena, explaining, 31
Next Generation Science Standards
   (NGSS). *See also specific practices*
   components, 11–12
   implementation, requirements for, 2
   instructional shifts mandated by, 94
   meeting, a vignette, 24–25
   resources and tools, 3

observation
   in the supervision cycle, 45*f*, 48
   theorizing, 59–60
   vignette, 58–59, 73
observation, elements facilitating
   implementation
   collaborative engagement, 72
   establish routines, 72
   incremental shifts, 71
   tensions, acknowledging, 71–72
   use a perspective of understanding, 69,
      71–72
observation tools
   the observation form, 62–63, 70*f*,
      123–124
   practice example, 63–69
   to prepare for the observation, 61–62
Obtaining, Evaluating, and Communicating Information. *See* Information, Obtaining, Evaluating and
   Communicating

Planning and Carrying Out Investigations.
   See Investigations, Planning and Carrying
   Out
Post-Observation Conference Worksheet,
   88–89

praise in feedback, 77–78, 82*f*

principals, 28–29

professional development

critical features in, 94

experiences and contexts, considering, 93–95

focusing on three groups for, 23–24

in the supervision cycle, 45, 45*f*, 49

theorizing, 93–95

vignette, 92–93, 106

professional development, examples

lesson adaptations, Analyzing and Interpreting Data, 103, 103–104*f*

lesson adaptations, generic, 100–101, 101–102*f*

science practice, generic introduction to a, 96, 97–98*f*

scientific modeling, introduction to, 98, 99–100*f*

professional development, planning for and implementing

aligning with supervision practices, 106

experiences and contexts, considering, 95–96

focus on one or one group of practices, 95, 105

using existing experts when, 105

Questions, Asking

defined, 13*f*

a feedback strategy, 78, 82*f*

instructional strategies, 125

key levers, 33–34, 33*f*

vignette, 17–19

resources, assessing for implementation, 47, 50

routines, establishing for implementation, 72

science

goal of, achieving the, 15

marginalization of, 2–3

student-directed and collaborative, 32

Science and Engineering Practices (SEP) skills, 2

science instruction

content-neutral approaches, 46

purpose of, 108–109

Science Instruction Observation Form, 62–63, 70*f*, 123–124

science practices

analyzing curriculum and instruction with, 23

content-neutral, 7

defined, 11

equity and, 14–15

implementing the, 40–41, 109–113

instructional elements for, 31

key levers, 32–34

theorizing the, 11–15

vignette, 9–10

science practices, three groups of. *See also specific practices*

focusing on for professional learning, 23–24

ISLP research study on, 16–17

working together, 16*f*

science practices classrooms, equitable, 14–15

Science Practices Continuum. *See also specific practices*

core elements of design, 31–32

instruction version, 29–31

supervision version, 29–31, 73

using, reaching consensus for, 39–40

sensemaking practices. *See also individual practices*

in the Continuum, 30*f*

focus of, 19

individual practices in, 16*f*

vignette, 19–21

skill/will matrix, 51–52

supervision

aligning professional development with, 106

content-neutral, 6–7, 46

in the Continuum, 29–31, 73

supervision—*(continued)*
  critiquing practices, 118
  differentiating in implementation,
    51–52
  evaluation, rubrics for, 46
  framework, theorizing the need for a
    science-specific, 28–29
  historically, 44–45
  investigating practices, 116
  sensemaking practices, 117
  subject-specific, 6–7
  vignette, 27–28
supervision cycle
  benefits of, 45
  theorizing the, 44–48
  using the, 46–47
  vignette, 43–44, 56
supervision cycle, stages of the
  feedback, 49
  illustrated, 45*f*
  observation, 48
  professional development, 49
supervision cycle implementation, elements
  facilitating
  admit vulnerability, 54
  beginning, 47
  build trust over time, 53
  differentiate support, 47
  foster collaboration, 54–55

supervision cycle implementation, elements
  facilitating—*(continued)*
  give permission for mistakes, 54
  leaders role in, 47–48
  maintain transparency, 55–56
  provide content-specific frameworks, 46
supervision cycle implementation, schoolwide approach to
  assess existing resources, 47, 50
  differentiating supervision, 51–52
  disruptions, 51
  leverage goal setting, 52–53
  preliminary planning, 50
  schedule each step, 50–51

teachers
  demands on, 1
  supports for, 1–2
tensions, acknowledging during implementation, 71–72
transparency in implementing supervision,
  55–56
trust, building during implementation, 53

Using Mathematics and Computational
  Thinking. *See* Mathematics and Computational Thinking, Using

vulnerability, allowing for, 54

About the Authors

Dr. Rebecca Lowenhaupt is an associate professor of educational leadership at Boston College. She earned her doctorate in educational leadership and policy analysis from the University of Wisconsin–Madison. A former middle school English teacher, she currently teaches aspiring school principals and superintendents. She has conducted research about the organization of schooling, principal practice, and instructional leadership. Her current study explores the role of educational leaders in supporting immigrant and refugee communities. She has received funding for her research from the W.T. Grant Foundation, the Spencer Foundation, and the National Science Foundation.
Twitter: @Rlowenhaupt
Website: www.rebeccalowenhaupt.com

Dr. Katherine L. McNeill is a professor of science education at Boston College. A former middle school science teacher, she received her doctorate in science education from the University of Michigan. Her research focuses on how to support students from diverse backgrounds in engaging in science practices as they make sense of phenomena. Through the generous funding of the National Science Foundation and the Carnegie Corporation of New York, she has worked on numerous projects focused on the design of curriculum, assessments, and other resources to support students, teachers, and instructional leaders in science practices.
Twitter: @KateMcNeill6
Website: www.katherinelmcneill.com

Dr. Rebecca Katsh-Singer is the science curriculum coordinator for the Westborough Public Schools (Massachusetts) and on the faculty at Brandeis University. She received her PhD in curriculum and instruction from Boston College, where her dissertation research focused on the beliefs and knowledge of district instructional leaders about scientific argumentation. Prior to beginning her doctoral studies, she taught elementary and middle school science for 10 years and worked as an instructional coach for science teachers. She has also consulted for research organizations and schools about science curriculum and done extensive professional development for teachers about the NGSS and science practices.

Twitter: @KatshSinger

Website: www.rebeccakatshsinger.weebly.com

Benjamin R. Lowell is a doctoral candidate in curriculum and instruction at Boston College. His research focuses on how teachers learn to teach science as a process of figuring out the natural world rather than a set of facts to be memorized. He is interested in professional development and preservice teacher education that supports teachers in shifting their vision of science instruction. Before beginning his doctoral work, he was a high school chemistry and environmental science teacher in the San Francisco Bay Area, where he also served as department chair and one of the leaders of districtwide professional development.

Twitter: @BRLowell

Website: www.benjaminrlowell.com

Dr. Kevin Cherbow received his PhD in curriculum and instruction from Boston College. His research focuses on how science teachers use curricular materials to craft instruction that is coherent and equitable for students. He is interested in working with teachers and instructional leaders to develop and maintain learning environments in which students see their science work as making progress on their questions and problems about natural phenomena. Prior to his doctoral studies, he taught 9th grade biology in New York City and served as an instructor for high school students carrying out biomedical research using animal models.

Related ASCD Resources: Instructional Leadership in Science

At the time of publication, the following resources were available (ASCD stock numbers in parentheses).

Effective Supervision: Supporting the Art and Science of Teaching by Robert J. Marzano, Tony Frontier, and David Livingston (#110019)

Engaging Minds in Science and Math Classrooms: The Surprising Power of Joy by Eric Brunsell, Michelle A. Fleming, Michael F. Opitz, and Michael P. Ford (#113023)

Engineering Essentials for STEM Instruction: How do I infuse real-world problem solving into science, technology, and math? (ASCD Arias) by Pamela Truesdell (#SF114048)

Leadership for Learning: How to Bring Out the Best in Every Teacher, 2nd Edition by Carl Glickman and Rebecca West Burns (#121007)

Lesson Imaging in Math and Science: Anticipating Student Ideas and Questions for Deeper STEM Learning by Michelle Stephan, David Pugalee, Julie Cline, and Chris Cline (#117008)

Making Teachers Better, Not Bitter: Balancing Evaluation, Supervision, and Reflection for Professional Growth by Tony Frontier and Paul Mielke (#116002)

Priorities in Practice: The Essentials of Science, Grades K–6: Effective Curriculum, Instruction, and Assessment by Rick Allen (#106206)

Priorities in Practice: The Essentials of Science, Grades 7–12: Effective Curriculum, Instruction, and Assessment by Rick Allen (#107119)

STEM Leadership: How do I create a STEM culture in my school? (ASCD Arias) by Traci Buckner and Brian Boyd (#SF114081)

Succeeding with Inquiry in Science and Math Classrooms by Jeff C. Marshall (#113008)

Teacher Evaluation to Enhance Professional Practice by Charlotte Danielson and Thomas L. McGreal (#100219)

For up-to-date information about ASCD resources, go to www.ascd.org. You can search the complete archives of *Educational Leadership* at www.ascd.org/el.

ASCD myTeachSource®

Download resources from a professional learning platform with hundreds of research-based best practices and tools for your classroom at http://myteachsource.ascd.org/

For more information, send an email to member@ascd.org; call 1-800-933-2723 or 703-578-9600; send a fax to 703-575-5400; or write to Information Services, ASCD, 1703 N. Beauregard St., Alexandria, VA 22311-1714 USA.

WHOLE CHILD
TENETS

1 **HEALTHY**
Each student enters school healthy and learns about and practices a healthy lifestyle.

2 **SAFE**
Each student learns in an environment that is physically and emotionally safe for students and adults.

3 **ENGAGED**
Each student is actively engaged in learning and is connected to the school and broader community.

4 **SUPPORTED**
Each student has access to personalized learning and is supported by qualified, caring adults.

5 **CHALLENGED**
Each student is challenged academically and prepared for success in college or further study and for employment and participation in a global environment.

The ASCD Whole Child approach is an effort to transition from a focus on narrowly defined academic achievement to one that promotes the long-term development and success of all children. Through this approach, ASCD supports educators, families, community members, and policymakers as they move from a vision about educating the whole child to sustainable, collaborative actions.

*The Instructional Leader's Guide to Implementing K–8 Science Practices relates to the **engaged, supported,** and **challenged** tenets.*

*For more about the ASCD Whole Child approach, visit **www.ascd.org/wholechild.***

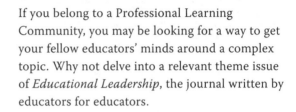

Town Mouse
Country Mouse

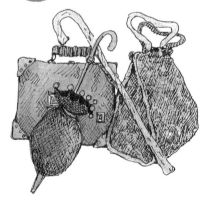

For Rosie
with love from Carol

Copyright © 1994 by Carol Jones
First American edition 1995
Originally published in Australia in 1994 by CollinsAngus &
Robertson Publishers Pty Limited

Library of Congress Cataloging-in-Publication Data

Jones, Carol.
    Town mouse country mouse / Carol Jones. — 1st American ed.
        p.   cm.
    Summary: A town mouse and a country mouse exchange visits and
    discover each is suited to his own home.
    ISBN 0-395-71129-0
    [1. Fables. 2. Mice—Folklore.] I. Country mouse and the city mouse. II. Title.
PZ8.2.J655To   1995
398.24 ' 5293233—dc20
[E]   94-14411
                                                                         CIP
                                                                         AC

Printed in China

                    10 9 8 7 6 5 4 3

CAROL JONES

Town Mouse Country Mouse

Houghton Mifflin Company

Boston

Town Mouse jumped up and down with delight. He had just received a letter from his cousin who lived in the country.

"Why don't you come and stay with me for a while?" Country Mouse wrote. "My cottage is on the edge of a field and I would love to show it to you."

"That's just what I need," Town Mouse said. "A rest in the country. Think of all that lovely food I'll be able to eat – fresh apples, homemade pies – mmm." His mouth watered at the thought of it and his tail twitched with anticipation.

Without wasting a moment, he threw a few things into a small suitcase and set off towards the country.

*T*own Mouse left the smooth city streets behind him as he walked out into the countryside.

He sniffed the clear fresh air. "My goodness," he said to himself. "This certainly is the life!"

With a contented sigh he sat down on a nearby rock.

"Get off me at once," cried an angry voice, as a tortoise popped its head out of its shell. "Who do you think you are?"

"Oh dear," said Town Mouse as he scampered off, "I do beg your pardon. I see there will be a few things I'll have to get used to in the country."

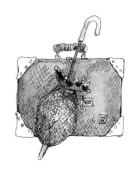

Town Mouse was very weary when he finally
arrived at his cousin's cottage.

"Welcome," said Country Mouse, who was very
pleased to see him.
"Come inside and rest. I'm just setting
the table for dinner."

Country Mouse's home
was warm and cosy,
and Town Mouse soon
forgot how tired he was.
He sank into a
comfortable chair.
Hungry from his long walk,
he dreamed of hearty country
food like blackberry pies and steaming hot bread.

Country Mouse's whiskers twitched with pride as he prepared the evening meal. He'd been saving up the dried peas and an apple core especially for his city cousin. How pleased Town Mouse would be to eat good country food.

Town Mouse's face fell when he saw what was for dinner. He tried not to think of all the delicious food he would be eating at home.

"Is this your usual meal?" asked Town Mouse politely.

"Well, the apple core is rather special, but I knew you would be hungry after your journey," replied Country Mouse.

Keep your
Whiskers clean

After dinner the two mice sat chatting happily
for some time, catching up on family news.
Town Mouse wondered what lay beyond the field.

Let's go for a walk in the forest," suggested Country Mouse.
A walk in the moonlight will help you sleep soundly.
But there can be dangers in
the country so stay close
to me."

Town Mouse soon forgot
how tired he was as
they set off across the
field. He watched the
frogs in the moonlight and
listened to the crickets
with delight.

Suddenly, there was a loud WHOOSH!
Town Mouse shivered with fright.

"Just keep very still," whispered Country Mouse. "It's only that big, brown owl looking for her supper. If we don't move she won't see us."

Town Mouse froze to the spot until the dark shape had flown away. He then turned and ran as fast as he could. He didn't stop to watch the frogs or listen to the crickets – he didn't stop until he had reached the safety of Country Mouse's cottage.

"Oh dear," panted Town Mouse. "There are so many new things I have to get used to in the country."

The next morning Country Mouse was up early cleaning his cottage, and collecting corn and berries for breakfast. Town Mouse's stomach grumbled as he thought about the honey-drenched toast and crispy cereal he would have been eating if he were at home.

"What lovely berries," he said, not wanting to hurt his cousin's feelings.

"Well let's go and gather some more for lunch," said Country Mouse, grabbing his basket.

As the two mice made their way across the field and through the farmyard, Town Mouse listened to the clucking of the chickens and watched the baby ducks as they waddled towards the river.

Suddenly there was a loud MOOO!

own Mouse looked into the two biggest, brownest eyes he'd ever seen. He didn't wait for his country cousin. He turned around and ran as fast as he could back to the little cottage on the edge of the field.

"I'll never get used to your way of life in the country," said Town Mouse. "Now that I have seen your home," he said to his cousin who had just arrived back, "why don't you come to town with me and see how I live?"

Country Mouse's tail flickered with excitement.

He quickly packed his bag and together the two mice set off.

The mice soon left the rough country roads and walked on down to the smooth city streets.

Country Mouse wondered at the huge buildings and admired the smooth pavements.

Suddenly there was a loud VROOOM! A big red car whizzed past the two mice, its tires hissing and its headlights blazing.

"Just stay on the pavement near me and don't step near the road," said Town Mouse. "You'll soon get used to the traffic."

Country Mouse shivered. How could anyone get used to these screeching monsters?

With his heart beating fast, Country Mouse ran
after Town Mouse, down one lane and up
another until they finally arrived at a large house.

"This is where I live," said Town Mouse, proudly
showing his cousin his home. "Come and I'll
show you the pantry. If we're lucky,
there'll be a rich, dark
chocolate cake."

"I've never eaten
chocolate cake,"
thought Country Mouse.
"I'm sure it's just one
of the things I will have
to get used to living in town."

own Mouse led Country Mouse out into a big room.
Their paws sank in the thick carpet. They scuttled
under a door and into a place filled with the most
delicious smells.

Country Mouse had never seen such food.
There was, indeed, a rich chocolate cake and
crunchy salted crackers and
a tantalizing slice of pie.

Country Mouse flicked
his whiskers over a
particularly juicy piece
of cheese.

Suddenly there was
a loud TWAAANG!

"*W*atch out," shouted Town Mouse, as he pulled his cousin aside. "Haven't you ever seen a mouse trap before?"

"N...no. Never," trembled Country Mouse. "We don't have anything like that in the country," and he sat down until he had recovered a little.

Suddenly the pantry door was flung open and in walked the biggest pair of brown shoes Country Mouse had ever seen.

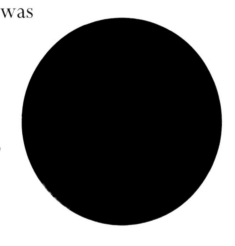

"Quick, we've got to run," whispered Town Mouse. "If he sees us, there'll be trouble."

The two mice zipped past the shoes, back across the soft carpet and into Town Mouse's home.

"Don't worry," said Town Mouse. "We'll go back to the pantry tonight and have a real feast."

Country Mouse wasn't at all sure he wanted to risk the pantry again. He thought longingly of his succulent berries and munchy peas and apple core.
But by midnight his tummy was rumbling, so the two mice set out again in search of a feast!

Country Mouse ran from one delicious treat to the next not knowing where to begin.

Suddenly there was a loud MEOW!

*C*ountry Mouse froze to the spot. A large black-and-white cat seemed to fill the pantry. His claws sparkled and his teeth snapped.

"I'll never get used to your life in town," trembled Country Mouse, and he took off just as the cat swiped a paw at him.

Country Mouse ran and ran and ran – out of the house, past the huge buildings and down the smooth city streets.

He didn't stop running until he felt the rough country road under his feet.

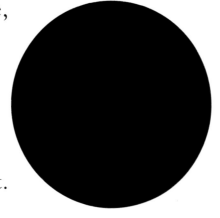